Copybook
Cricket

Copybook Cricket

The Guide to
More Success and Enjoyment

Les Lenham
and
Ralph Dellor

 Robson Books

First published in Great Britain in 1989 by Robson Books Ltd,
Bolsover House, 5-6 Clipstone Street, London W1P 7EB

Copyright © 1989 Les Lenham and Ralph Dellor

British Library Cataloguing in Publication Data

Dellor, Ralph
  Copybook cricket.
  1. Cricket. Manuals
  I. Title II. Lenham, Les
  796.35'82

ISBN 0 86051 488 9

Printed in Great Britain by Billing & Sons Ltd, Worcester

CONTENTS

INTRODUCTION

There is no shortage of cricket coaching books on the market. In fact, from the time cricket became an organized sport with recognized teams and a formal structure, there have been many instructional books accredited to star players and numerous official coaching manuals. All of them, at different levels, are designed to tell you the correct way to play the game. They aim to take the place of the coach. Not everybody can have a personal coach on demand, but they can keep the book handy to provide instant information about the right method. Coaching, however, is not just about telling players how to bat, bowl or field. It is also about analysing the faults which creep into everybody's play and, having identified those mistakes, eradicating them.

In this book we hope to give you the full picture. Of course you will want to know the correct method, but you will also want to know where you are going wrong. It is one thing to know what to do when faced with a straight ball on a good length. Virtually any book you pick up will tell you to play a forward defensive and give you detailed instruction as to how this stroke should be played. You then go out to play your innings, the first ball you receive is straight and on a good length, so you play forward defensively. You think you have done exactly what the book says and yet your off stump is leaning back at a drunken angle. Where did it all go wrong?

We hope that in the pages which follow you will find the answer. You should be able to run a replay through your mind of the shot you have just played and look at it objectively. You will probably find that you have made one or more of the common mistakes associated with that particular shot. Once you know what you are doing wrong, it just becomes a matter of concentrated practice to put it right so that you don't do it again. For the average player, the chances are that the fault lies in something simple. Remember the old adage: the great players are those who do the basic things better than anyone else.

When it comes to ironing out the problems, some of the advice might seem a little strange at first. However, persevere because you might well have started to do something correctly that has always been wrong before. Quite soon the right way should start to feel natural and then the improvements in your play should become evident. Of course, you will need to check that you are following the advice correctly. Make sure you fully understand the information that is being given before moving on. If you don't get the gist of what is being said first time, read it again until you do. It might also be worth your while to read sections which do not necessarily apply to your speciality. It is a good idea for a batsman to know how a bowler is thinking, while bowlers can learn a lot by understanding the batsman's problems.

Remember, in all cases we are offering guidelines. Some are firm, because there is little room for individual interpretation. Others, which apply to areas of the game where personal preference can be allowed a fuller rein, are looser. Some people would have you believe that cricket is a game for automatons. It is not. Without the scope for individuality, cricket loses much of its charm. If there were only one way to bowl, there would not be the widely divergent actions that have brought success at the highest level. Some elements of those actions are common to all; individuality accounts for the rest. We hope you will find that our approach to coaching caters for such individuality without undervaluing the all-important basics. The objective must be to improve your performance. If you play better and have more success, the enjoyment you get from the game will increase accordingly.

This improvement will not just happen on its own, or even from reading this book. You must really want to succeed, for only then will you devote the practice time that is so essential. When you read something in these pages that appears to apply to your game, go out and put the theory to the test. With dedicated and constructive practice of the right type, you will surely achieve the consistent success which leads to the lasting enjoyment we want you to get from this wonderful game of cricket.

Les Lenham and Ralph Dellor

BATTING

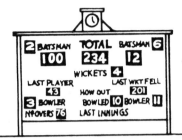

PREPARING TO BAT

The suggestion that in order to play an innings in August you ought to start preparing as early as April may sound like one of those little japes usually associated with the first day of that particular month. However, April is often the time when players get their kit together for the new term, and it is then that the foundations for a successful season can be laid.

It goes without saying that you need to get the best protective equipment you can afford. If you have your own, and care for it properly, you will not find yourself in the situation that has befallen so many of us at one time or another. We all know the feeling when we are due to go in next, rummage through the club kit bag, and find two left-handed pads with three straps between them. That hardly puts a batsman in an ideal frame of mind to go out and play a controlled innings.

The choice of a bat occupies the mind of a cricketer for many hours before a purchase is finally made. There are many reasons why an individual will decide on a particular make and model. But 'It is cheap', or 'It's the same make that Viv Richards used when he made his last Test century', or 'The colour of the manufacturer's label matches the club sweater' are not among the best reasons for selection. Far more important are the weight and the pick-up. The two things are not necessarily connected. A light bat might pick up badly, a heavy one will often appear to fly into the backlift. A good guide is to pick the bat up with your top hand and go through a repertoire of imaginary strokes. If you cannot manage that, the bat is too heavy for you. A three-pound log might be fine for a professional with arms like pistons, but the average club player will just not be able to use the same piece of willow effectively. So try the one hand test, and consider whether you might not be better off with a lighter bat.

Once decently kitted out, you are that much closer to actually batting. If you are next man in, you will probably be feeling nervous, to a greater or lesser degree. Be aware of the difference between being keyed up and eager for the contest and being anxious. It is one thing to have the adrenalin flowing in healthy anticipation, quite another to be rigid with fear. So how can we overcome a bout of nerves that prevents us from playing at our best?

Nerves are really caused by fear of failure, and can be eliminated if a batsman has confidence in his own ability to cope with whatever is bowled at him. Such confidence will come if you know you have prepared in the best possible way for the innings ahead. This preparation includes the right type of practice, to say nothing of the right amount of practice. It is a sad fact that cricketers as a breed tend not to practise as much as they should. Even top golfers before playing a championship round, will go out on the practice ground and hit dozens of balls. Gary Player, the great South African golfer, was once accused of being a lucky player. 'That's right,' he replied, 'and the more I practise, the luckier I get!'

If you take pride in your personal performance on the field you will want to know that you have taken every opportunity to practise before a game. Great players such as Tom Graveney, Ken Barrington and Geoff Boycott would try to have a net every day. Barry Richards asked for fifty balls to be thrown at him to practise a certain shot. Roy Marshall liked to spend ten minutes that had the bowlers picking up every ball. That meant he was hitting straight. Sunil Gavaskar, one of the world's great opening batsmen, was noted for an immaculate defensive technique. Yet, at the end of a net session he would spend some time smashing straight sixes. He appreciated the importance of practising all aspects of his game so as to be totally prepared for any situation he might encounter.

Not all club players enjoy the same opportunities as these star batsmen. But there is no reason why anybody should not get in as much practice as possible. Make the most of your club net sessions, arrange others if time and facilities allow, and even use the time before you go in to bat. Get someone to throw a ball at you so that you get used to going forward to a few, then back. Ask for the type of delivery you want and keep going until satisfied that you are moving properly. It is helpful to have a net or wall behind the person throwing at you. You can then hit the ball hard and this will increase your confidence as you assume a feeling of power.

There are a couple of other little tips which will help ensure the right preparation for an innings. When about to go in, try to sit in the same type of light in which you are going to bat. The glare in the middle will be very difficult to deal with if you have been sitting in the shade of the pavilion. And however much money you have resting on the outcome, never sit glued to the 3.30 at Newbury moments before you go in to bat! It is a far better bet to sit watching the bowling and making up your mind how you are going to play against it. Watching for indications of the speed of the pitch and how much bounce certain bowlers are getting. This, in turn, will enable the better player to programme himself as to whether to think back or forward. Against a medium pacer who keeps the ball well up, the batsman will be thinking of going forward. On the other hand, a quickie who is banging most balls in short will have a batsman programmed to go back on release of the ball. This can be adjusted when he has had the opportunity to judge line and length.

Openers will not have had the opportunity to sit and mentally prepare for the battle ahead at their leisure. The first time they get a look at the bowling is when the first ball is on its way. But they can go out before the game and look at conditions. They can take a ball out and drop it to see how much bounce there is in the pitch, and even throw a couple to each other to get some idea of the pace. Later batsmen can get reports from those just dismissed, even if these only confirm your own observations. No batsman ever misses a straight ball! He will usually give you a lurid account of lift and movement merely to cover his own inadequacies.

When your turn comes to go in, make sure you approach the wicket in confident manner. Stride out as if you own the place. When you get to the middle ask for your guard in a similarly assured way. You might still feel nervous, but if it doesn't show you won't be boosting the bowler. Which guard you take will largely be governed by your height. The idea is for the batsman to have his head over middle stump when in the stance position. So a tall man bending into a conventional stance will need to take a leg stump guard, while his 5 foot 4 inch counterpart will be nearer middle. If you adopt the more upright style of stance you will probably want to take middle stump so that your head is in line with the stumps as you face up. This is something you can check for yourself by looking in a mirror—an underrated but vital piece of self-coaching equipment.

You are now almost ready to face the first ball. Before you do, look around the field and take a mental note of where the fielders are positioned. With a fine leg and backward square leg out, you will not be thinking of going for a hook, while the man posted deep at mid-off prevents you from going for the lofted drive, at least early in your innings. Remember, take as long as you want looking round the field and doing any necessary, or even unnecessary, 'gardening'. It is your prerogative to set the pace of affairs before facing the ball.

PLANNING AN INNINGS

Thinking batsmen will usually be more successful than those who go out to the middle with nothing more going through their minds than a vague notion that it would be good to score some runs. Of course, every ball has to be treated on its merits, but a batsman can still have some overall plan as to how his innings is going to be played.

The openers and, if they fail, those going in early in the innings obviously have more time to formulate their plan. The captain will usually have some idea of the target he is seeking at the outset. This will be based on conditions, the strength of his team and his assessment of the opposition. Batting last, the target is determined by the scoreboard. In general terms, the task of the openers is to make a solid start, gradually prising the initiative from the fielding side. The speed at which they do this is determined by the time available. So, in a five day Test a score of 60 for no wicket by lunch on the first day is acceptable. In a 40 over match such a scoring rate will attract few plaudits, at least from those supporting the batting side.

As the innings progresses, the plan of an individual's innings becomes rather more determined by the situation. It does not need a great cricketing brain for number eight, going in to face the last over of the innings for the side batting first in a limited overs match, to score as many as possible. But even then he can have a plan. If he is a pusher and nudger, with a well set big hitter at the other end, he will be thinking about getting a single to leave the pyrotechnics to his partner. Where are the spaces in the field into which he can push that single?

When there is time to construct a planned innings, it is best to set yourself small targets to achieve. A century is a long way down the road, but milestones along the path make the going easier. So the first target must be getting off the mark. Then you want to reach double figures. Having reached that point you look for 20, then 30 and 40, until a half century is within reach. The same method can be used when playing out time. Stumps can seem an eternity away when, in mid-afternoon, the scoreboard reads 30 for 6 chasing 280 to win. Going for the draw, you set yourself still to be there a quarter of an hour later and keep going in that way. This is where batting partnerships in the true sense are so valuable. The two batsmen should meet at the end of every over to encourage each other. 'Well done, that's another one gone. Keep it going. Watch for the one that goes the other way from the bowler at my end,' or that sort of thing, can do wonders for confidence by letting the other chap know he is not on his own out there.

However the innings is projected, it is important to remember that all plans have to be flexible. You might be going for a four an over target when a bowler delivers the over of a lifetime. All six balls are on the spot and doing a bit. Getting out to the sixth ball when trying to hit the four required in that over is hardly helping the team's cause, especially if you would have done well merely to have got a bat on that ball. It is easier to score six from the last over with four wickets in hand than it is to score a hundred off the last twenty overs with three wickets to fall. The only target that really matters is the final one.

PLAYING WITHIN LIMITATIONS

We would all like to be able to stroke a ball through the covers for a boundary like Donald Bradman. However, if in reality we play the cover drive like Donald Duck we would probably be well advised to leave that shot in the pavilion until we have worked on it a bit. You should know your limitations as a batsman and not give your wicket away by letting the bowlers exploit a weakness. Instead, play to your strengths and spend time eradicating the weaknesses. This means that you will need a good repertoire of shots if you want to maintain the initiative, along with a good positive attitude. You might have a difficult time early in your innings, but you can still keep the board ticking over by 'fidgeting' for runs. Keeping alert, calling well and playing controlled shots into the gaps can soon put 20 up against your name while you are finding your feet in the middle.

TIMING

Timing is a magic word in batting, yet how many really understand what it means? In scientific terms it might be defined as a seemingly inverse ratio between the power of the shot and the effort applied. In cricketing terms it means that the ball streaks off towards the boundary even though the batsman has used no apparent effort. Three considerations can help you achieve timing in your play.

Allow the ball to come right up to you. You will be surprised just how long you can stand still before moving as the ball comes towards you. Several first-class batsmen have either thought or actually said to themselves, 'Hold on, hold on' as the bowler is about to deliver. Having assessed the line and length of the ball, they then make one positive movement forwards or backwards into line. The front foot plunger who infests so much of our cricket is rarely a good timer. He needs an accurate bowler who can regularly hit the middle of his bat!

If you steel yourself to keep still until the very last moment, you will then move quickly with an explosive movement. Even your defensive shots will be well timed as you play them as a last resort. By thinking positively you will be looking to attack every ball. If you have to change from a 'fetch that' to a 'get past that' frame of mind because the ball demands it, you will find that your defensive shots, too, have a positive crispness about them.

Another secret of timing is to get speed in the hitting zone. Again, that sounds rather technical but all it means is that the bat should be travelling quickly at the point where it is going to strike the ball. It should be accelerating into this zone from an easy swing. To achieve this, you must have a backlift. Some people advocate using a low backlift early in the innings but such a move smacks of a negative approach. Get the bat high and get it there early so that from the very outset of your innings you can hit the ball hard and with timing.

The third rule of timing is to stay down in the shot. The easiest way to destroy timing is to be anxious and come up too early. Keep your head down in the hitting zone and go through with the shot. A good technique will obviously help and this should be achieved as we progress through the book.

THE SET-UP

Before we get to the point where we actually hit a ball, it is essential that the batsman has a good set-up. This expression means that you are holding the bat in the correct manner, picking it up straight, and keeping the head still and the eyes level.

If you watch a top-class professional golfer preparing to drive off the tee, you will notice that he goes through a little routine to ensure that he is giving himself the best possible chance of hitting the ball as he wants. He lines himself up and makes sure that he is gripping the club properly. He does this every time he addresses the ball, even though it is just waiting there to be hit from exactly the required spot. Surely it is worth a batsman going through a similar routine before playing each ball? If it is important for a golfer to prepare thoroughly to hit a stationary ball, it must make sense for a batsman to get it absolutely right before he has to deal with a ball bouncing towards him at anything up to 90 miles an hour.

So many times a batsman gets himself out because he does not grip the bat in the correct manner. The Vs formed by the thumb and forefinger on each hand should be in line with a point midway between the outside edge of the bat and the middle of the splice. Beware of letting the top hand slide too far round the back of the handle. If this happens it will prove almost impossible to play the drive and any effort which is made will almost certainly be dominated by the bottom hand. This in turn causes the bat to come down across the line of the ball, with all the associated problems that fosters. It is impossible to stress too much the need for a firm top hand grip. It is not a bad idea to imagine yourself strangling the handle with your top hand. Do it correctly and you will feel a cohesive firmness running from just below the elbow, down your forearm, through your top hand into the bat handle. One other point on hands. It is a mistake to have them too far apart on the bat handle. Nothing makes it easier for the bottom hand to take over control. Keep your hands close together and they should work together.

Having taken hold of the bat in the prescribed manner, we now have to lift it up. A fairly straightforward action, you

A sound grip.
1. A strong top hand indicated by the back of the hand facing towards mid-off.
2. The back of the thumb on the bottom hand faces square on the off-side

A basically sound grip ruined by the hands being too far apart on the handle and the Vs not in line.

Side view of a sound grip with good alignment of the Vs formed by the thumb and forefinger on both hands. It is only when in this position that the hands will work together.

A disastrous grip. The hands are too far apart, the top hand cannot be dominant in this weak position, and the bottom hand has crept too far round the back of the handle.

A good backlift, straight over the middle stump.
1. The head has remained upright with the eyes level.
2. The front elbow is pointing straight down the pitch.

The side view of a good backlift.
1. The head is slightly forward.
2. The back elbow is away from the body.
3. The front forearm is parallel to the ground.

This backlift has drifted round towards fine leg and, unless major adjustments are made on the way down, will result in the batsman playing inside out.

If the bat is picked up towards third man it cannot be brought down straight without a big loop.

A poor excuse for a backlift. The hands have not been lifted up and the bat has only been raised by the cocking of the wrists.

A typical but awful stance.
1. The batsman's head has been allowed to fall over outside the line of the stumps and too much bending at the waist means that the eyes are no longer level.
2. His feet are far too open and out of alignment with an imaginary line from wicket to wicket.

might think. It should be, but as you look around you will see batsmen in Tests and batsmen on the village green trying to make life difficult for themselves. Given that we want to bring the bat straight down, it would seem to make sense to pick it straight up. But no. For some reason known only to them, some batsmen insist on taking it back towards third man, or even fine leg. To bring it straight down from that position they need to have a loop in the swing. Why add complications?

While we are considering the backlift, beware of one other bad habit. Don't let your bottom hand do the work. Instead, use that strong top hand to push the bat back and over middle stump. And get those hands high. Cocking your wrists from the stance position is not a backlift. If you get your hands above your waist and the toe of the bat above your hands you will be able to get a good, full swing. Any lower than that minimum and the chances are that you will try to force your shot and lose timing, power and shape.

Now that you are holding the bat properly and picking it straight up, what else is there to consider in the set-up? The answer to that is simple. Your head. You will never see a good

The heavily built man will have to come up in his stance to get his eyes level.
1. The bat has come up off the ground.
2. His toes are slightly out of alignment but his back foot has remained parallel to the crease with the front foot opening out a little to allow the left-hander a better view of the bowler.

batsman moving his head about as he prepares to face the ball, nor one who does not have his eyes level. You will see plenty of bad ones with their head cocked to one side and nodding around like one of those dogs seen in the rear windows of cars. Work it out for yourself. The ball is generally delivered from a point about seven feet above the ground. As, or before, it reaches you it will have reached ground level. It might well have swung laterally as well. This means that there has already been plenty of movement across your visual plane. Bob your head about and you can double that movement, and make it harder to react to it. Your head must be still if you want to get the best possible sight of the ball, while your eyes must be level. If you want to look carefully at something—some small print or a distant object—the way to get the best view is to keep the eyes level. A batsman with a ball hurtling towards him should be pretty keen to get a good look at it and so he should keep his eyes level, or parallel to the ground. In that way they will work together and give a far better chance of focusing on the ball. The focus is ruined if his head is on one side. Test it for yourself. Rest one ear down on your shoulder and look intently

A bowler's view of a good stance.
1. The batsman is standing tall with his head over the line of the stumps and his eyes are perfectly level.
2. The front elbow has been released from the body and is pointing straight down the pitch.
3. The top hand is close to the top of the front pad.
4. The knees are relaxed and the toes parallel to the line of the stumps.
5. The base of the bat is just behind the toes of the back foot.

at an object on the far side of the room. Stay in that position for a full minute. Then straighten up and look at the same object with your eyes now level. You will feel them dropping into focus.

It might well be that to get your eyes into a good level attitude you have to stand a little taller in your stance than is usually the case. There is nothing in the laws of cricket which states that you must have your bat touching the ground before executing a stroke. Some critics frown at the idea of a batsman standing straight at the crease as he prepares to face, but what is wrong with such a stance? The essentials are that he grips the bat correctly, picks it up straight, high and early, and stands sideways-on with his head still and eyes level.

As for the stance itself, remember that it is the platform from which all your strokes begin. Obviously, as you are going to

The side view of a good stance.
1. The batsman's head is slightly forward.
2. The feet are comfortably apart on either side of the popping crease.

play most of these strokes from a sideways position, you might just as well start out sideways. This holds good whether you are adopting the conventional stance or an upright one. The idea is for you to be balanced so that you are in a position to move either right back or right forward. To do this you will want to be relaxed, knees slightly flexed, feet comfortably apart and with your weight evenly distributed. If you go for the conventional stance with the bat on the ground, position it just behind the toes of your back foot with the bat face slightly angled in towards your pads. Your hands should be resting on your front thigh, just about in line with the crease on your trousers. From this position you will be able to get it up early into that high, straight backlift we have already considered.

Another point to bear in mind when taking up your stance does, quite literally, concern a point. That point is formed by a prominent front elbow jutting out towards the bowler. Your front shoulder will also be pointing that way, with your head tilted slightly forward. From here you will find that you retain that sideways position much more easily as you move into the shot.

JUDGING LINE AND LENGTH

It was once said that the judgement of line and length was the key to technique. Without this judgement you might be capable of playing the most perfectly executed shots, but they will count for nothing unless you can assess quickly to which ball they should be played. Now there are several aspects of cricket where a small tip can be the key to success; a word here and a slight adjustment there can often make the world of difference to a player's performance. But there is no such magic formula for learning to judge line and length. The ability to do this stems from just one thing—practice. It would be nice to be able to offer a short cut but, quite simply, there is none.

It all begins with a small boy playing with his enthusiastic father in the back garden. In his formative years the lad is simply encouraged to whack the ball anywhere. This is the fun side which gets him hooked on the game. From about the age of seven or eight he begins to get taught some basic technique, like the grip, stance and backlift. Now he can be encouraged to play some proper shots. Father tosses the ball up to him and the boy takes the natural step forward to play the ball. From the moment he has any success in doing that, the boy is subconsciously programmed to move forward to that length ball in future.

Having reached this important stage, the shorter ball is thrown in. The usual response is to move back and give it a cross-batted whack. Provided the boy takes a good step back towards the wicket to play it, that is just what is wanted. He is playing a rudimentary pull shot and, more importantly, he has learned to move forward to some balls and back to others. Every time he introduces a new shot, the father/coach should mention the length and line of the ball against which it is played. In this way the boy begins to appreciate the importance of the correct response to any ball, and from this point improvement depends on the amount and quality of practice he is prepared to put in.

Geoff Boycott was a perfect example of how a player improves through dedicated practice. He realized early in his career that he was not blessed with the same natural flair which was the hallmark of some of his more flamboyant contemporaries. To keep up with them he had to work harder on his game, and he worked to such an extent that in terms of figures he left most of the so-called natural players behind.

It is never too late to start practice, but the later you leave it the more you will need to make up for lost time. Furthermore, make sure that you practise in a thoroughly constructive manner. Unfortunately, most club net sessions begin as nothing more than exercise and degenerate into playtime. Bowlers rush in and try to bowl as fast as they can without any thought of accuracy. Batsmen attempt to hit every ball into the next parish. If they just slog, judgement of line and length becomes unnecessary.

Net sessions should be used for a specific objective. You should be aiming to improve on past performances. If you can ask someone to throw or bowl you a certain type of delivery, all well and good. If not, either stay behind with a friend or arrange a separate session in which you can be thrown or bowled that length and line of ball. If, for instance, you want to work on your drive you might only get two or three half volleys in your turn batting in the net. If you fail to recognize one, miss the second and edge the third you have not made much progress. With a ball thrown on a consistent length, you can really improve the shot. Having grooved the execution, finish the session by having different length balls thrown at you so that you can learn to select the correct type of ball against which it should be played.

That is sensible practice. The more of it you get, the better you will be able to make a quick and accurate judgement of line and length and you will become a better player. Allied to a good technique, this judgement will enable you to respect the good ball but give you time to punish the bowler when he errs. That must be the basis of good batting.

FACING THE FAST MEN

There is nothing in cricket to match the spectacle of a fast bowler steaming in to let go his thunderbolts. Nothing, that is, unless you happen to be twenty-two yards away in the firing line! Yet fast bowling is only one of the challenges a batsman has to overcome and, granted that he faces the challenge in a way that gives him the best possible chance, there is no reason why he should not make a brave effort at coping with the task in hand. Apart from the necessary guts and determination, what is going to give him that chance?

When facing genuinely quick bowlers, there is a lot to be said for 'thinking back'. When the ball is speeding towards the batsman he will need as much time as available to play it. By moving back, using the full depth of the crease, you can effectively lengthen the pitch by a full yard. Pace bowlers would give their eye teeth for an extra yard of pace and here you are with the opportunity to take a yard off his pace. This does not mean that you move back before having an opportunity to judge line and length. It means that you are in your stance with your weight on the front foot. You are now in a position to move back rather than forward as soon as you have seen the right line. If, however, you find the ball is well pitched up, having moved a long way back you can still come right forward into the shot. In effect, you will then be playing only just in front of your crease, but you will not be playing a 'big shot'. You will get into trouble trying to hit the ball too hard. If driving, use the pace of the ball to provide the power; if defending, aim for a technically sound forward defensive shot.

Having decided that you are probably going to move back, it is essential that you keep sideways-on. To begin with, this offers the smallest possible target for the bowler to hit if he is bowling at your body. More importantly, you will be in a better position to play the ball. So many batsmen get out because they have found themselves turned front-on as they go back. Inevitably the bat comes down across the line of the ball and it takes immense skill (and even more luck!) to get the bat crossing the line at exactly the same moment as the ball arrives. From a sideways position the bat comes straight down, and the longer it is on the line of the ball, the more chance there is of making contact.

It is good to have a high backlift whenever you play and whatever type of bowling you are facing. Against fast bowlers it is vital. There is a lot of nonsense talked about lowering your backlift when facing quick bowlers. Provided your backlift is straight, it should still be high. If the ball bounces more than you expect, you will be in position to play it down if your hands have been high. If you have low hands and the ball lifts, you are guaranteed to push up at it.

It is sometimes said that a high backlift against the faster bowlers makes a batsman more vulnerable to the yorker. However, provided the high backlift is also a straight backlift, it is easy to slam down on the ball and keep it out of your stumps. It is when you are trying to slam down from a backlift out towards third man that your problems begin, and end!

Obviously you will be helped by fast reactions and even the occasional bit of luck when facing the fast men, but above all else you need confidence. Go out into the middle and react like a rabbit caught in the glare of the headlights, and the result will be much the same. You are likely to get splattered! If you tackle the job boosted by the confidence which comes from having a definite plan, you will probably not only survive but flourish. You are likely to have more time to play a shot than you might imagine. Mentally, you need to keep on top of the situation and prepared to react to the ball. You are thinking of going back, and if the ball is going to hit the stumps you will play a backward defensive. If it is climbing way over the stumps you will sway out of the way and let it pass harmlessly by. If it is wide and not climbing too much, you will attack it.

Armed with this confidence in your own ability to deal with whatever comes your way, you should be able to survive at the crease. In the early stages of your innings that is all you are trying to do. You want to stay there without taking undue risks, letting wide ones go whenever possible. These merely act as sighters so that you can get used to the pace and bounce. As you gauge conditions you can begin to expand, moving away from the strict percentage game as you blossom. If you can just hang on at the start of your innings, you will be in a position to take on the quicks as they tire. You will be reaching your best as they pass theirs.

PLAYING THE TURNING BALL

'Oh good! They're bringing on the spinners.' How often do you hear those words said on the pavilion balcony as batsmen waiting to go in discuss a bowling change out in the middle? It matters not a jot that the man just taken off was an erratic opening bowler of no great pace and even less control. The fact that a spinner is coming into the attack is greeted with unrestrained glee. This is despite the fact that most batsmen score more freely against the ball coming on to the bat than against a style of bowling which demands that they take the initiative to keep the scoreboard moving. They have to look for a ball which is of poor length and/or off line to punish, while playing the good ball safely.

The first question is 'Which way is the ball turning?' First we shall consider the off-spinner—the bowler who turns the ball into the batsman from the off. A glance at the section dealing with off-spin bowling (page101) will give you the key to what he is trying to do. On a turning pitch he will be attacking. He will be aiming to pitch the ball outside the off stump so that if the batsman misses, he hits. So many batsmen make life easy for the spinner by missing too often.

The first rule is to stand still. There should be no forward or backward movement until the ball is in the air and on its way towards you. It is the speed of the pitch which governs whether you will then be 'thinking' of going forward or back, but never make the movement until the ball has been released. On a slow turner you will be thinking of going on to the back foot as often as possible. This will give you extra time to see exactly what the ball is doing off the pitch. On anything quicker you should be looking to get forward as much as possible to give the spin less time to take effect.

When the ball is turning appreciably, the right-hander must eliminate thoughts of scoring on the off-side if the ball is on a good line and length. You might get away with it, but you are taking unwarranted risks. It is better to look for ones and twos on the on-side, thereby not taking on the spin but helping it along its way.

Early in your innings, particularly, you will be looking to survive without ever missing scoring opportunities. So how best to do this? Against a good length ball the answer is the forward defensive. You can find details elsewhere about the technicalities of playing the shot, but there is one very important feature when playing it against the off-spinner. You play a conventional shot but, almost as an afterthought, you should ease your back foot across as a secondary line of defence. It is not defence against a turning ball but against one that doesn't turn. After your front foot has landed and as you are playing the shot, that back foot slides along the crease towards point. Against the floater or arm ball you might well get an outside edge. Normally this would go to slip or the keeper, but by getting the back foot round behind the ball, any edge will go into your pad and not into eager hands. If you do make contact with the middle of the bat, at the completion of the shot that ball should roll slowly out on the on-side of the pitch.

All the time you should be looking for the bad ball so that you can wrest the initiative from the bowler. For instance, the minute the bowler overpitches, you must be looking to drive. Once again, mistakes occur when you try to play against the spin, so you will be looking for gaps on the on-side or straight, but no wider than a straightish mid-wicket.

Once you have settled in and have adjusted to the pace, bounce and turn, you can use your feet to manufacture half-volleys out of good-length balls. Do not be over-zealous in your pursuit of the off-spinner until you have got the measure of his repertoire. There are so many batsmen who have a look at only a couple of deliveries before they see the red mist. They go charging off down the pitch, head bobbing up and down, and invariably arrive near the pitch of the ball in a hideously contorted position. They might get away with it once or twice, but they never really take command. You must be looking for total authority. If you have gone down the pitch to drive but find that you have been deceived in the air, there is no penalty for adjusting to a defensive shot. It might not be what you had in mind when you set out from the crease, but there is no disgrace in merely thwarting the bowler's plan if you cannot execute your own. It is pretty frustrating for him to lure you down the pitch, see you beaten in the air, only for you to recover the situation from him.

If the off-spinner bowls a good-length ball but allows his direction to stray so that the ball is missing leg stump, you can employ the sweep. Also, remember that attacking fields can be destroyed by hitting the ball over the top. When aiming to go over the infield, it is very important to go right through with the shot. A full swing of the bat is vital if you are aiming to hit a six. Like so many aspects of the game, this is not going to happen on its own. If you expect to go into the middle one day and hit the spinner over the top, you will probably come unstuck. Practice will make you proficient. Spend the last few minutes of a net session against a spinner in a constructive way. Do not just slog; practise hitting sixes in the correct way.

Not all the bad balls an off-spinner bowls will be over-pitched. On a turning pitch, especially, he can try too hard, pull the ball down when trying to spin it too much, and you are presented with a very hittable delivery. Provided it does not bounce too high, you can force it off the back foot. Again, the rule is to play it with the spin. Forcing against the spin is bound eventually to make a bad ball a wicket-taking delivery.

If it is dropped very short, a further option presents itself. You can play the pull shot, aiming to hit in front of square. Only if it is both very short and very wide of the off stump will you consider cutting. Playing this shot against the turning ball is fraught with danger. However, if the match situation demands, such risks have to be taken.

While the predominant thinking is to get forward whenever possible, there are going to be occasions when you are forced to defend against the short ball. When you play the backward defensive on a turning pitch, you can just open up your position slightly. With the ball turning in from the off, this will allow you to play with the spin, to tuck the ball away past the short legs for ones and twos.

When the off-spinner gets on to a pitch that does not offer very much turn, he will be forced to employ other weapons. Instead of looking for bite off the pitch, he will employ more subtle flight in an attempt to beat you through the air. He will vary his line of attack, using the width of the crease, and is likely to bowl more floaters. The batsman will still be thinking forward, but with the ball turning less dramatically he will be widening his target area to drive straighter. This target will now encompass an arc from wide mid-on to extra cover. However, even when the ball is not turning it is a mistake to attempt to drive too square.

Bearing in mind the fact that the bowler will be employing the arm-ball more frequently, great care must be taken when sweeping. You must be certain that the ball is pitching outside leg stump before attempting the shot. Otherwise it might drift back in the air to trap you leg before.

Going back, keep sideways-on to defend or, if there is low bounce, to force the ball into the same arc as for the drive off the front foot. Using your feet to make the ball into a half-volley, you can, in this instance, hit over mid-off with a degree of safety. If the ball should turn more than expected or if you allow too much bottom hand to come into the shot, all that will happen is that the ball will go a little straighter than expected.

Of course, on a pitch that does not offer the off-spinner very much help, he may opt to fire the ball in at leg stump with a 6/3 on-side field. You will then be looking to drive on the leg side. Once the line becomes less tight and the bowler strays to leg, you can come forward and despatch the ball over mid-wicket. This demands that you hit up right through the ball with a full shot. Because you allow a little more right hand to come into the shot than usual, it is often a good shot for the less gifted player to employ. Provided, that is, the bowler has not stationed a man at deep mid-wicket. Do check the field before you offer catching practice to the man out on the boundary!

Again, the sweep can be used when the off-spinner takes up this line of attack, while the leg glance off either front or back foot can be extremely profitable. Once you are well set, you might even consider giving yourself a little bit of room to drive into the arc between mid-off and extra cover.

To vary his line of attack on a turning pitch, the off-spinner may well decide to go round the wicket. As well as presenting you with extra problems, he is giving himself more opportunity to get an lbw decision. To counter this line, open your stance slightly by turning your front foot towards cover instead of point. The back foot must stay square to enable the pick-up to be straight, but the front shoulder comes round to give you a better sight of the approaching bowler. Again, your back foot will edge across towards point so that you are in a position, whenever possible, to hit the ball back in the direction from which it came.

Sweeping must be undertaken only with the utmost caution. If a ball pitching on the stumps turns, it will be straightening at just the right angle to go on to hit the wicket. That, after all, is why the bowler has gone round the wicket in the first place. Therefore you have to be quite certain that the ball is pitching outside the leg stump before attempting to sweep.

Even on a flat surface which is not offering very much turn, the off-spinner will sometimes experiment by going round the wicket just to vary his line of attack and make the batsman think. When he does, it opens the off-side as a run gathering area. You are not now looking to work the ball wide on the leg-side, otherwise you will be playing against the angle of delivery. At the same time you must guard against playing too wide on the off-side or you will be playing right across the line. To counter the straighter angle of attack, you can still edge round and be looking to play back into the V between mid-on and mid-off whenever the opportunity presents itself.

So far we have dealt with the ball that turns into the right-handed batsman. When facing the bowler who turns the ball away from the right-hander, there is a new set of problems to overcome and a new strategy for scoring runs. We are talking about the orthodox left-arm spinner and the leg-break bowler, both with the ability to deceive the batsman with a ball that goes in the other direction. The left-armer has his arm-ball which drifts in towards the batsman, while the leg-spinner will occasionally surprise you with a googly—the off-break delivered with what appears to be a leg-spin action.

On anything other than a slow, wet pitch the batsman should be programmed to go forward as often as possible against an accurate bowler of this type who keeps consistent line and length. Needless to say, you have to establish the line and length of each delivery before making the move. And once again, the later you can play, the more time you have to judge the qualities of the ball. On a slow pitch, the batsman who gets into a good sideways-on position will be better served by thinking back and playing the ball off the pitch.

When faced with the good length delivery pitching on middle stump and turning to the off, the batsman will be forced to play forward defensively. In order to allow for the ball to turn on to the bat, do not play directly to the pitch of the ball. If it is pitching on middle stump, you should be playing forward on off stump.

Just as you did when playing an off-spinner, you will be aiming to drive the over pitched delivery. The difference is that, with the ball turning away from the bat, you should now be looking to drive between mid-off and extra-cover. By now you will appreciate that you are once again aiming to play with the spin and not against it. With the ball spinning away, you have to concentrate hard on leaning into the drive. Unless you do, you will find yourself giving catches off the outside edge as you go one way and the ball turns the other. If the bowler overpitches on leg stump, do not try to drive against the spin to mid-on. Instead, aim straight or even play between the stumps at the bowler's end and mid-off.

Once you have played yourself in and are sure of an even bounce, a ball pitching outside leg stump can be swept. You cannot be given out lbw to this delivery, so make certain you have your pad positioned as a secondary line of defence in case you fail to make contact with the sweep. Even though you will be hitting against the spin, the very short ball can be punished with a pull. You will need to be a technically sound puller to bring it off with a regular degree of success, and make sure you are striking the ball towards mid-wicket rather than behind square.

Short-pitched deliveries on the stumps can be forced through the off-side from off the back foot. When either forcing or defending on the back foot it is important to establish a very sideways-on position. If you have opened up, with a backlift going out towards third man, the bat will come down a line almost guaranteeing that you will end up playing against the spin. When the ball is short and well wide of the off stump, you can play the square cut. At least, you will be able to play it if you have lifted the bat up straight in that sideways position. If you take it out towards third man, you will end up just playing a little chop or, worse still, developing a tortuous loop as you bring it down.

THE LEFT-HANDED BATSMAN

Most coaching manuals will show right-handed batsmen playing the strokes and suggest reversing the position for left-handers. The fact that a majority of cricketers bat right-handed makes it logical to illustrate the text with batsmen of that style. However, the problems facing left-handed batsmen are not just a mirror image of their right-handed counterparts.

The left-handed batsman has always had to cope with the difficulties created by a right-arm bowler operating over the wicket. That is a far more common situation than a right-hander dealing with a left-arm over. It means that the ball is angled across the batsman and he has to adapt his technique to deal with this line of attack.

A top-class left-handed batsman will realize that a right-arm over delivery pitching on a good length, middle and off, will not hit the stumps unless it straightens after pitching. Yet while he is safe from getting bowled or lbw from such a delivery if it does not come back into him, he is particularly vulnerable to the edge to wicket-keeper or slips. To counter this angle, it is helpful to move the back foot across the crease as a first movement immediately the ball has been released. As you make this movement, slightly close the right shoulder by turning it towards the off. In this way you will keep in a sideways position in relation to the angle of delivery. When moving on to the front foot to deal with the over pitched delivery on leg stump or middle and leg, the left-hander should beware of trying to drive it too wide on the leg. Instead, look to play the ball into the V between extra-cover and mid-on.

Since most bowlers are right-arm over merchants, their follow-through creates rough outside the left-hander's off stump. Any ball pitching in this area is liable to do something unpredictable. It is one more problem for the left-hander to guard against and counter. Even though he will be trying to play as late as possible, he must pay attention to the line of the ball as early as possible. He does not want to be defending his wicket against a delivery pitching in the rough area that would not have hit the stumps.

To ensure that he is sideways-on to the right-arm over the wicket bowler and that he gets a good sight of the ball, he needs to adjust his stance position slightly. The left-hander should have his back foot parallel to the crease, but with his front foot slightly open. From this position, and with that initial back foot and front shoulder movement, he should be in perfect shape to overcome his particular problems.

RUNNING BETWEEN WICKETS

This is an aspect of the art of batting in which any one of us can be as good as the very best Test cricketer. Or perhaps it would be more accurate to say that any two of us can be as good as the very best pair of Test cricketers, for running is a two-man job. When you watch two batsmen with a good understanding and confidence in each other's calling, notice how the fielding side begins to look ragged. No end of runs can be picked up by good running, which can prove just as effective at moving the score along as the most elegant cover drive. On the other hand, there is nothing more frustrating to a batting side than losing a wicket to a run-out. There are seldom circumstances in which such a dismissal is excusable as it can usually be put down to bad cricket. There are plenty of ways the fielding side can get you out without offering them unnecessary assistance.

Calling has to be the basis for good running. There are only three calls—'Yes', 'No' and 'Wait'. If the call is 'Wait', it should be followed by a 'Yes' or 'No' to avoid any doubt between the batsmen as to what either of them are intending to do. Please note, the call of 'Sorry' should have no place in cricket's vocabulary when it comes to running between wickets!

As a general rule, it is up to the striker to make the initial call if he can clearly see where the ball has gone when he has played his shot. So, anything in an arc from a squarish mid-wicket to backward point comes within the scope of the striker. When the striker is in no position to see where the ball has gone, the non-striker makes the initial call. Whoever does make the call, the other batsman has the right to veto a call of 'Yes'. The non-striker might see the ball going down to fine leg and call for what appears a simple single. What he might not have seen is the striker slip as he plays the shot. If the striker thus feels he is in no position to make the run, he should counter the call of 'Yes' from the non-striker with his own firm 'No'. The non-striker should then respond immediately.

Remember, the calling should be loud and clear. Apart from the fact that a call which is inaudible to your partner is totally useless, a loud call can do wonders for your confidence. And while it gives you a boost to hear yourself letting out a resonant call, the fielding side realizes that it has a confident opponent on hand.

As the batsmen cross in the middle of the first run, they can indicate further possibilities to each other. Comments like 'Look for two' alerts your partner that there might be a second run available. It should not be left at that, for a further call is necessary once the first run has been completed. It is usual for the batsman with the best view to make the second call, but again the other man has the right of veto, especially when he is running towards what is likely to be the danger end. A supplementary call of 'Your end' keeps up the communication and lets your partner know that the throw is coming in to the end towards which he is running.

In most instances the striker will run down the side of the pitch from where the bowler has delivered, with the non-striker using the other side. However, if the batsman's weight has taken him to the side on which the non-striker is backing up, he will probably find it easier to continue along that path. In this case, the non-striker has a responsibility to give him plenty of room by going wider and eliminating all possibility of a collision. The same applies when batting with a left-hander. Having plotted a course, stick to it by running straight. There is little point in running round a circular course when it is so much quicker and easier to run straight from A to B. Needless to say, you want to run each run as quickly as possible. It is surprisingly easy to pick up extra runs by taking those quick singles and turning ones into twos, and easy twos into well-judged threes. Run stealing is not just a phrase for poets.

The correct way to back up when there is a right arm over the wicket bowler. The non-striker has a clear view of the bowler while he is moving down the pitch with his bat still in the crease.

One of the problems which sometimes creeps into running is the failure of the batsmen to keep watching the ball. Even when backing up, the non-striker should be in a position to get the best possible view of the bowler. So, with a bowler operating over the wicket, the non-striker should be backing up with the bat in his left hand. Thus he will be able to leave his bat in the crease while walking up the pitch in readiness to run when the bowler has released the ball. By the time the shot has been played, the non-striker should be a couple of yards up the pitch, but ready to get back in should he need to. If a right-arm bowler goes round the wicket, the non-striker should back up with the bat in his right hand to be able to get in the optimal position for a run.

Once you are under way in the run, you still want to keep the ball in view. So, if the batsman has pulled the ball through mid-wicket, the non-striker runs with the bat in his left hand. This will allow him to turn at the other end while watching the ball

Because the non-striker did not change hands when he completed the first run he is in no position to assess the possibility of a second. He is sliding his bat in correctly, but it is in the wrong hand. This means he loses ground while trying to look at the fielding activity in the covers.

The correct way to complete a run. The batsman has a good view of the ball and is sliding in the bat from some way short of the crease.

and the fielder chasing it. As he comes back for the second, he should change hands so that the bat is being carried in his right hand. Again, he will be able to keep the action in view as he reaches the bowler's stumps. Meanwhile, the striker will have carried the bat in his right hand on the first run and swapped it to his left on the return.

On the completion of a run, never crash the bat down as if you are swotting an ant. Slide the bat in at full arm's length and turn for the second run. Even if you have no intention of going for another run, it is good to get into the habit of making your ground as soon as possible by sliding the bat in. All these points save fractions of a second, but those fractions count. It takes about three seconds to complete a run. This means you cover a yard in 0.15 seconds, so a fraction of a second saved represents a fair distance on the ground. Most run-outs are by no more than a yard, so it is worth paying attention to every means of saving time.

If the worst comes to the worst, and you realize that you are about to be run out, never give up. The only thing that looks more stupid than a batsman run out by half the length of the pitch is a batsman, half a pitch away from safety, with the ball on its way to the wicket-keeper, who gives up running, only to see the keeper fumble the ball and run him out at the second attempt. Even when the cause looks hopeless, do everything you can to get in. Merely doing so can put extra pressure on the fielding side and that might cause the error which lets you back in. Remember, you are not out until the umpire raises his finger.

BACK FOOT PLAY

There is one sure sign of a class batsman. When he goes back to the short ball, he goes right the way back. It is a yardstick which has endured over the years, for it has been a feature common to the play of all the great batsmen that when they move back, they use the full depth of the crease. Conversely, when you see a batsman apparently riveted to the popping crease when dealing with a ball pitched short of a length, you know he is going to struggle. Furthermore, when you do move back, you want to keep in a sideways position so that your front shoulder is always pointing towards the bowler.

Remember, cricket is a sideways game, so how do you ensure you stay sideways on as you move back?

It is essential to establish a firm base. This can be achieved by moving the back foot back parallel to the crease. The front foot is then slid close to the back foot so that you find yourself in a position of natural balance. The only time you deviate from this sideways position is when you go back to a ball pitching on the line of middle and leg or leg stump. In this instance, while the back foot still goes back parallel to the crease, the front hip is allowed to be turned slightly open. This might sound extremely complicated and more suited to a book on anatomy rather than cricket. However, all you are doing is slightly turning to give yourself a better sight of the ball coming towards your legs and giving yourself room to bring the bat down on to it. To deal with such a ball you never move back outside leg stump. If you do and you miss it, there is a grave danger that the ball will crash into your pads and from there on to the stumps.

THE BACKWARD DEFENSIVE

This is the shot to employ when faced with a delivery pitching short of a length and threatening the stumps. If there is no danger of the ball hitting the stumps, you should not be playing a defensive shot in the first place. Bearing in mind you are going to get no runs from a defensive shot and you cannot get bowled or lbw if the ball is going to miss the wicket, what is the point of defending against a harmless delivery? Play it perfectly and you get no runs; play it badly and you might get caught. The formula does not appear attractive as we weigh up the percentages.

However, once we have judged the ball to be threatening the stumps from short of a length, the backward defensive is the shot to use. Having already established the need to move back, using the full depth of the crease, you want to ensure that you go back down the right line. You know that you never go back outside leg stump, and that you are not going to defend against a ball too wide of the off stump. So, within the danger channel, you are going to move your back foot into a position just inside

An impregnable backward defence.
1. Head right in line with the ball, and standing tall.
2. The front elbow has risen with the bounce so that the ball is played with the middle of the bat.
3. The top hand is in control and the bottom hand has relaxed.
4. A firm base has been constructed by the back foot going back parallel with the crease while the front foot has been drawn back close to the back foot.

The batsman is too open and consequently has played right across the line. The ball has taken off stump and yet the batsman has pushed across towards mid-wicket.

Side view of the correct way to play back defensively.
1. The head is left tilting forward.
2. Control in the hands has allowed the bat to stop close to the body and angled slightly down.
3. He has gone back using the full depth of the crease.

the line of the ball. Were you to leave it, it would pass over the ends of your toes and under your chin. This means that you have got your head perfectly into line and have left room for the bat to be brought straight down close by your still sideways body.

As well as getting your head into line, you will, of course, want your eyes level, with your head tilting slightly forward. In effect, as you have moved your feet and body backwards towards the stumps, your head is just 'left behind' a little. Batsmen sometimes get into trouble pushing up at the ball as they go back. They could eradicate that fault by getting the head to lean forward towards the bowler. From a high, straight backlift they would then be in a position to bring the bat down on to the ball so that they meet it close to the line of the body. This does not mean that you should play a cramped little shot somewhere in the region of your hip pocket. You should play

This batsman has problems, but not uncommon ones.
1. The bottom hand has pushed through to send the ball upwards.
2. The open base has caused him to play across the line.

the ball just in front of your body so that you can still see the ball right up to the moment of contact with the 'sweet' part of the bat—in the middle of the blade where the bat is at its thickest.

More trouble is in store if you do not have your top hand in control right through the shot. Allow the bottom hand to take over and you will find yourself popping up catches as the bat is pushed through, angled upward. Instead, make sure you play with the top hand just in advance of the toe of the bat. This angles the bat down while the face should be square on to the line of the ball and never turned so that the ball angles off towards the leg or off. You can reduce further chances of giving those fielders catches if you allow your bottom hand to relax into a forefinger and thumb grip as you play the ball. In this way you are making sure the top hand is still the dominant one and, should the ball find the edge of the bat, this 'soft' bottom hand grip acts to cushion the ball rather than adding to its impetus towards the slips. But ideally the ball will have come off the middle of the bat. This being a defensive shot, that is where the ball has hit the bat rather than the bat hitting the ball. With your head still upright, you should be in a position to watch the ball roll gently away along the ground as you look at it through the bat handle, as it were. Allow your head to topple over so that you are looking round the bat handle and you will be off balance and out of control.

To sum up the vital elements of the backward defensive:

1. A high, straight backlift.
2. Move right back and into line in a sideways position.
3. Bring the bat straight down on to the ball, slightly angled down but square on.
4. The top hand is in control throughout, with the bottom hand relaxed.

If one of these elements is missing, you will have to make adjustments as you play, and against the quicks, there is not much time on offer!

THE FORCING SHOT

Once a batsman is accustomed to conditions and is set, he can consider taking more aggressive action against the short-pitched delivery by forcing it through the field for runs. That is provided the ball has not bounced more than the height of the stumps. If you try to force it when it bounces higher than that, you will encounter problems in keeping it down and playing with control. Similarly, if you do not go back the full depth of the crease you will not have time to play the shot, and find yourself of more interest to the scoreboard operator dealing with wickets fallen than the one putting up runs.

In essence you want to concentrate on the same elements as you did for the backward defensive stroke. You take up exactly the same position from which to play. The difference now is that from the highest point of the backlift you apply more acceleration to the bat as it comes down, and at the point of contact the bottom hand firms up to give some extra power to the shot. Instead of trying to drop the ball dead at your feet, you now allow the bat to continue through the hitting zone, with your arms extending through the line of the ball in the direction where it has been hit.

It is a mistake, especially against the quicker bowlers, to try hitting the ball too hard. So many batsmen get out to deliveries which do not really deserve a wicket because they go back and

The batsman has failed to use the depth of the crease, the front foot has gone out to the on-side, thus leaving him very open. He has played the ball a long way from his body because he failed to move back into line, hence the catch to slip.

The recipe for disaster.
1. The head has come up.
2. The bottom hand has pushed through across the line.

The way to play a forcing shot off the back foot.
1. The head is tilting forward.
2. The top hand is in control with a firm grip.
3. The right arm has extended through the ball with the bat pointing towards extra-cover, the direction in which the ball has been hit.
4. A firm base has been created by correct foot movement. The back foot has stayed parallel to the crease to maintain a good sideways position.

To strike the ball past mid-on, the front foot has opened out a little, as has the hip. However, the back foot moved back parallel to the crease in order to help the initial sideways position. Again, the hands are going through in the direction of the ball.

try to whack the ball into the next parish. They lose balance, control, and their wicket. It is so much better to use the pace of the ball on to the bat for your power. Provided you have struck the ball crisply, you do not need a full follow-through. You can check the bat at the completion of its swing through the hitting-zone. The bat face should be pointing towards the heavens, the bat will be pointing straight down the direction in which the ball should now be racing to the boundary. As your arms have already extended through this line, the bat becomes a continuation of your top forearm, with the bottom arm more or less straight. Against slower bowlers you might need a full follow-through. This time, instead of checking the swing of the bat, you allow it to continue through the arc so that now it finishes with the handle pointing after the ball. It saves time if the fielders can follow the line from your bat to find the ball in the long grass beyond the boundary!

THE PULL

Winning cricket is all about cashing in on the opposition's mistakes. Given two sides of roughly equal ability, the side which induces its opponents to make the more mistakes and then takes advantage of them will win. This being the case, when the bowler makes the mistake of bowling short, from just outside off stump to a yard outside leg, you want to be sure of taking the four runs on offer.

It is essential to select the right delivery in the first place. Don't make the mistake of trying to play the pull from very wide of the off stump. It is far better to cut such a ball. And make sure the ball is not bouncing too high. Once it is lifting above the level of your shoulders, you should be deciding whether or not to hook rather than playing the pull.

Perhaps the most common mistake made in the scoring of four runs is attempting to play the shot without a high backlift. We are going to play the pull to a short ball. Short balls tend to bounce higher than those of full length. Therefore, if you hope to play the ball down, you have to be hitting down on to it. If you try to pull a short ball with a low backlift you are almost guaranteed to be hitting it up and so giving the chance of a catch. That is, if you hit the ball at all. Unless you play from a high backlift there is every chance that you will be playing a cramped little swat at the ball and will fail to make any contact.

Remember, as in all the back foot shots, you want to use the full depth of the crease as you move back into position to give yourself as much time as possible in which to play the shot. While you are getting into the right position as far as going back is concerned, you also want to ensure you are getting into line with the ball. In this instance, getting into line means just that. The only way to play this shot successfully is to get in a position so that if you miss the ball with your bat, it will hit you smack in the middle of your chest! But there is little to worry about. If you move right back and get fully into line, you should always hit it provided you keep watching the ball. There is a tendency for some batsmen to turn their head to look in the direction where they hope the ball will go before they hit

The batsman has got too far inside the line of the ball. It should be hitting him if he misses but he will be fortunate to make any contact here as he chases it down the leg-side.

it. Please wait until after you have completed the shot before turning to see where it has gone. The ball only needs to bounce unpredictably and, if you have already started surveying the leg-side boundary, you will have a bruise rather than four runs. Keep watching the ball right on to the bat so that you can adjust to any variation in the bounce. If you then hit the ball as intended there will be no need to turn your head to see where the ball has gone.

As with all shots, it is important to be in a balanced position to pull with any degree of consistent success. If you are toppling off balance you will be in no position to be in command of your shot. To create this position of balance you want a firm, wide base. This is a quick-footed shot, so you are almost dancing into position. The back foot moves back, and the front foot is taken back the same distance as the back foot and thrown out towards square leg. As you move back into this position, with your chest square on to the bowler, your head is left tilting forward just as when playing the backward defensive. If you allow your head to be thrown back there is no way you can be balanced. If you are not balanced, all the old problems of timing or even making contact at all will become evident once again.

At the completion of the shot, your weight should have been transferred from the back to the front foot—the one that has been thrown out towards square leg. You are hitting out that way and so it makes sense to get your bodyweight moving in the same direction. Perhaps the word 'bodyweight' should be underlined, because it is only your weight and never your head which moves. Those eyes are always rock-steady behind the ball. All we want is the weight that, at the start of the shot, is on the back foot to be transferred to the front foot on completion. The precise moment for such a change is determined largely by the pace of the bowler. Against slow bowlers you have time to transfer your weight as you play. Against the quicks you will have played the ball before the weight transfer takes place, but your weight still ends up on that front foot.

If you ask most batsmen where they are aiming to pick up their four runs from the pull, they will tell you 'just backward of square'. This is why so many short balls outside leg stump are wasted. If you try to hit the ball too fine down the leg-side, you will probably have taken up a position inside the line before trying to catch the ball up as it passes by. That is far from easy, for the bat then has to be travelling faster than the ball and has only a fraction of a second in which to complete the

The batsman has failed to throw his front leg out to the leg-side, his weight is still on his back leg so, as he is leaning back, there is every chance that he will hit the ball upwards.

catching up. It is far better to aim in front of square. If you make good contact, the ball will go where you intend; if you are a little late on it, it will go fine.

One more point: you should make contact with the ball at a full arm's stretch. Short-armed jabs belong in the boxing ring. On the cricket field it is far more profitable to bring the bat down in a long arc from a high backlift. The power and timing come from your extended arms; the shot will lack both if you are cramped for room. Playing this correct way, you will find that you do not have to hit the ball too hard. Once again the pace of the ball coming on to the bat provides the power. Remember, if you merely help the ball over the boundary you will get four runs. If you smash it across the boundary, through a hedge and to the far side of a car park, you still only get four.

So, to sum up the correct way to play the pull shot:

1. A high backlift.
2. The back foot goes a long way back while the front foot is thrown out towards square leg, bringing your chest on to the bowler directly in line with the ball.
3. Your head is left tilting slightly forward as you go back and keeps still throughout the shot.
4. Having hit the ball at full arm's stretch between square leg and mid-wicket, your weight finishes up on the front leg.

A well-executed pull, where the ball has been struck down from in front of the body.
1. The head, about to turn, is still looking at the point where contact was made.
2. There is good arm extension.
3. There has been a good transfer of weight on to the front foot after the batsman went back in line using the full depth of the crease.

THE HOOK

To hook or not to hook? That is the question. Had Shakespeare—who was qualified by birth to play for Warwickshire—been a cricket fanatic, he might well have faced this problem. The answer in most cases has to be not to hook. Very few should attempt what is admittedly a spectacular shot when it comes off. Furthermore, at the lower levels of the game it is seldom necessary to contemplate it, for few bowlers or pitches have the pace to provide the ball for such a shot. Even when the ball is bouncing head high from short of a length, the shot is so laden with risk that only the best batsmen in the right circumstances should consider it.

This is a well played hook.
The body has pivoted and the
ball merely helped on its way.

The batsman has decided
against hooking. He has
swayed out of the way safely,
keeping his eyes on the ball
and dropping his hands to
keep the bat out of trouble.

This time the batsman has
ducked under a lifter but has
once again kept looking at the
ball and has kept his bat right
out of the way.

Not the way to avoid trouble. This batsman has taken his eye off the ball as he ducked and left the bat up like a periscope. The ball could have hit him or his raised bat and there is nothing he could have done about it.

If you decide to take on the fast bowlers and play the hook shot, you must not attempt it too early in your innings. You need to have judged the pace of the pitch and got your eye in, for even the best batsmen programme themselves not to go for it too soon. Never hook the new ball or a very fast bowler on a quick pitch. Having made the decision to have a go, there will be plenty of opportunity later on rather than going after it as soon as you get to the crease.

Once you are well set and conditions are favourable, you still have to ensure that you are hooking the right line. If there is lateral movement off the pitch, you have to dispel thoughts of hooking anyway, for you can never be certain of the right line at the speed the ball is coming. The line you are looking for is leg stump or just outside, so that there is no difficulty in moving just inside the line. Then, if you miss the ball, it will pass harmlessly above your front shoulder.

Over the years there has been a great myth circulating in the game as to how it is advisable to hook down. You can pull down, but it is a total fallacy to suggest that an 80 mph delivery lifting head high can be hit down. In fact you are not really hitting it at all. All you are doing is helping it on its way, having got into the right position.

Most players should decide that the hook is too risky for them. So how do we lesser mortals counter the fast, lifting delivery? If it is straight, our first thought must be to move back to play a backward defensive. Then, should the ball not get up as expected, we are in a position to play it. However, once we have established that it is a vicious lifter, it is time to take evasive action. Sway inside or outside the line, or duck underneath it, but always watch the ball. Never turn your head away and always keep the bat out of harm's way. If you leave your bat waving in the air like a periscope, the ball might well hit it and give a simple catch.

THE LEG GLANCE

There is one other shot you can play to the short ball on the leg side. It is not as spectacular as the hook or as productive as the pull, but it is a pretty useful weapon in the batsman's armoury. The leg glance is played to a ball which is short of a length, on or just outside leg stump, and bouncing not much above hip height.

To play it properly, you move back into line and let the ball come right up to you. The top hand must be in control at the moment of contact, while the bottom hand comes in slightly to close the face of the bat, glancing the ball backward of square leg. Problems await if you are tempted by a ball passing too wide of the leg stump. If you prod out at it, there is a danger that the bottom hand will come in to push up at the ball and send a catch to men waiting round the corner for such an error.

Once again, there is a danger in trying to hit the ball too hard. You do not want to force it or, worse still, flick at it. Let the pace of the ball on to the bat do the work for you, just turning it away for ones and twos. The most common reason for making poor contact or even no contact at all with a leg glance is closing the face of the bat too early. You are not trying to apply power to the ball, so you can concentrate on the timing. Only a slight closing of the face is necessary to angle the ball down and away for those runs which keep the board ticking over in perfect safety.

The glance off the back foot.
1. Because the head was left forward it is helping the batsman to direct the ball downwards.
2. The high front elbow is compensating for the bounce of the ball.
3. The top hand is totally in control, just shutting the face to direct the ball on to the leg side.
4. The batsman has gone a long way back and allowed the ball to come right up to him.

Not much more could have gone wrong with this glance off the back foot.
1. The head has fallen right over to the off.
2. The bottom hand has taken over, pushing through too far.
3. His back foot has gone too far to the off, balancing the faulty head.

THE SQUARE CUT

When the bowler drops a short ball well outside the off stump, it can be punished with the square cut. The ball must be wide of the stumps, however, for if it is too straight you will find yourself getting cramped for room and very likely give a top edge to the waiting slips or wicket-keeper.

By now you will have realized that a low backlift is one of the basic faults associated with all shots, but the importance of a high backlift is patently obvious for the square cut. Unless the ball bounces so high that the shot should not be considered, a high backlift ensures that you are bringing the bat down on to the ball which will then travel downward without any danger of a catch.

At the first-class level some batsmen give themselves room to play this shot by pulling away from the ball as they make contact. They finish with their weight on the front foot. This is because they seldom encounter deliveries on such a wide line to play a conventional cut. However, making room in this way can lead to extra problems. Any unpredictable bounce or deviation finds the batsman out of control and unable to adjust. It is far better if, at the completion of the shot, all your weight is taken up on the slightly bent back leg. You are then in total control and will be hitting down on to the ball, gaining more power without extra effort. Associated with this movement of the back foot well back and across should be a turn of the front shoulder. Naturally you want to use the full depth of the crease and get across to the ball, and turning your front shoulder round towards cover point as you move has two beneficial effects. The first is that, as your shoulder turns, your top hand is being pushed back higher and straighter. The second is that you are building more power into the shot without having to hit the ball so hard that you fall off balance.

Despite this turning and moving back and across, it is a mistake to try to cut too fine. Remember it is called the square cut, and it should be aimed just in front of square as you play the shot with a full extension of the arms.

This ball is too close to the off stump to cut effectively. The batsman has got tucked up and will not be able to play a controlled shot.

More common faults. There has been no use of the crease to get right back and the batsman has pulled away from the shot so his weight has not finished totally on the back foot. In this position he has little chance of making any contact.

The basis for a good square cut.
1. As the batsman goes back he is turning his shoulder, winding up the
spring which will put power into the shot. The bat is at just about the
highest point in its backlift.
2. A sound base is provided by the back foot going back and across.

Good contact has been made with this square cut.
1. The batsman has hit down at a full arm's stretch from a high backlift.
2. The back foot has gone back and across to take up the batsman's weight.

The golden rules of cutting are:

1. A high backlift so that you are cutting down.
2. The back foot must go right back and across.
3. As you move back and across, the front shoulder turns so that it points towards the covers and you are watching the ball over that turned front shoulder.
4. Aim just in front of square, playing the shot at full arm's stretch and finishing with your weight on a bent back leg.

A delicate late cut.
1. He has kept his head over the ball.
2. After a turn of the front shoulder he has slightly rolled his wrists to keep the ball down, with the control resulting from the use of his hands.
3. The batsman has used the crease to move right back.

A late cut fraught with danger. With hands as low as this there is little doubt that the batsman will cut under the ball.

THE LATE CUT

When the short, off-side delivery is a little closer to the stumps, that most delicate of shots, the late cut, can come into play. The old pro's used to talk about never cutting until the end of May. It was probably the late rather than square cut which they had in mind because it can be a risky shot if the bounce is anything other than totally predictable. Consequently it is not a shot to be played early in your innings before you have had a chance to gauge the bounce.

Many of the elements associated with the square cut are to be found in the late cut, and many of the same mistakes creep in. You need a high backlift to ensure you hit down on the ball, and as you do so you can just help the ball downward with a roll of the wrists. In the square cut this happens naturally, but with the late cut, where you are only using the pace of the ball as it passes, a little extra help downward does not come amiss.

You need to go back a long way as you take that initial step, but you will not need to go far across. Remember, this shot is being played close to the off stump. If you go across too far you will get cramped for space. And having got into the right position you then need plenty of patience. Hurry this shot or try to belt the ball and you will probably have ample time to dwell on your mistake in the pavilion. Wait for the ball to come up to you. Delay your shot until the last moment.

FRONT FOOT PLAY

One of the most widespread faults in cricket is the plunge on to the front foot before the batsman has had a chance to judge the line and length. Watch batsmen across the entire spectrum of cricket and eighty per cent of them have an initial movement on to the front foot. It makes life so much easier for the bowler if he knows where the batsman is going before he bowls. Meanwhile, the batsmen in question are giving themselves quite unnecessary problems. If they merely plant their front foot forward down the pitch, as so many do, they either have to hope that the bowler obliges by pitching it up on the line to which they have committed themselves, or make totally unwarranted adjustments in order to cope.

Even when the type of bowling and the condition of the pitch demand that you programme yourself to think forward, you have to stand still to judge the line and length before committing yourself on to that front foot. You cannot make this judgement until after the ball has been released by the bowler. Even then you must let the ball come up to you before making one positive forward movement. Never shuffle forward early so that you find yourself waiting for the ball to arrive.

Some years ago every schoolboy who played cricket was indoctrinated with the idea of getting his foot to the pitch of the ball. Such utter nonsense has produced our nation of front-foot plungers. It is possible to get your foot to the pitch of the ball without ever getting your head in line or over the ball. If the coaches who went round with their meaningless parrot-cry about the front foot had instead insisted on their charges leading out to the ball with head and front shoulder, there would now be a lot better batsmen around.

Going forward on to the front foot is so much easier if you wait for the ball to be released to judge the line and length. Keep still as the ball comes to you before leading on to the line with your head and front shoulder, and stay in a sideways position so that an imaginary line from your right hip bone through your left would be pointing straight down the pitch. If this line points towards mid-wicket, you have opened up and become chest-on to the bowler. Do this correctly and notice where your front foot lands: in the correct position. Get everything else right and the foot moves naturally. Plant your foot alongside the ball and it does not follow that everything else is right.

THE FORWARD DEFENSIVE

This shot is used to counter a good length ball on a line threatening the stumps. By now you know that you do not play a defensive shot to a delivery too wide to hit the stumps, but how do you define 'a good length'? In effect, it is a ball pitching in that area which leaves some doubt in the batsman's mind as to whether he should move forward or back. Much shorter and he would know immediately to go back. A fuller length becomes a half-volley or full toss. A straight ball pitching in the area, causing doubt in the batsman's mind, is exactly what the bowler is striving for when trying to find a 'good length'. As such it is the most dangerous ball a batsman has to face, and so it is rather important that he has a sound defensive technique to combat the danger.

You might well find it surprising to encounter a high backlift among the requirements for a good forward defensive stroke. Why is a high backlift necessary if all you are trying to do is to stop the ball hitting your stumps? The answer is that until you have seen the ball in the air you do not know you are going to play defensively. Every batsman should think positively and be looking for scoring opportunities. It is only when forced to do so by the quality of the delivery that we defend.

While it is therefore important to get the bat up early, there should be no other early movement. Fielding close to the wicket, you could sometimes hear batsmen saying 'wait, wait'

A very solid forward defensive shot.
1. The head and front shoulder have led on to the line of the ball and the head is now in advance of the front knee.
2. The top hand is in control, angling the bat down.
3. The back leg is not bent. The heel is off the ground but the foot is parallel to the crease.
4. The weight has all been taken up by the bent front leg.

to themselves as the bowler was in his delivery stride. They were just reminding themselves that they must not commit themselves too early, and it is a ploy that could still be used with some purpose. Having waited to see the line and length and having decided that the ball demands a forward defensive shot, you then lead out on to the line of the ball with the head and front shoulder close together. Keeping the shoulder in close proximity to your chin ensures that you stay sideways and that you get your head over the ball. And you want to keep your head upright rather than falling over to the off-side of the pitch as so often happens.

It is important to maintain this head position for a number of reasons. We have already noted that leading out with the head

The bowler's view of a sound forward defensive.
1. The head is perfectly over the line of the ball.
2. The ball has been met in the middle of the bat and not too low.
3. The front foot is pointing towards extra-cover to provide a firm base.

and front shoulder will get you on to the right line to play the ball. Your front foot automatically then goes into the right place, with the weight taken up on a bent front knee and the back leg almost straight. This all helps to get your weight forward and over the ball. If you leave your trunk too upright there is every probability that you will push up at the ball instead of playing it down. There will be problems too if that head drops over, for then you will lose balance, the bottom hand takes over and you prod across the line of the ball. Remember, the longer the bat is coming straight down the line, the more chance you have of hitting the ball.

One more point about the positioning of the front foot. While it should land in exactly the right place if you have moved correctly, you must pay a little attention to where it is pointing. If it points straight down the pitch you are likely to overbalance. If it points towards extra-cover, even when playing on the leg stump, you have a good firm base. Meanwhile, the back heel can be allowed to come up off the ground, but it should never pivot round towards the off-side. If it does so, you will destroy the sideways shape, your hips will turn round pointing towards mid-wicket, and once again you will find the bat coming across rather than straight down the line.

Another means of ensuring that your head is over the ball as contact is made with the full face of the bat is to get your head down. It is the full face of the bat that the bowler should see as you play forward defensively, and never your full face. If the bowler is looking more at the top of your head as you play the shot, you are getting your head into the right position. You want to get as far forward as possible, for the closer you get to the ball as it pitches, the less opportunity it has to deviate. However, there are limitations to the distance you can move forward. Unless your head is in advance of the front knee, you will find it impossible to get over the ball. You will sit back, your head will come up and your bottom hand pushes through. This leads to a closing of the bat face, mistiming, and giving room to be bowled through the gate between bat and front pad which opens up as you strive to retain balance. Given all those things that can go wrong, it is advisable to get into the right shape!

With all this emphasis on playing the ball down, you must still guard against playing too low. Some batsmen look as if they are getting down on to their hands and knees as they play forward defensively. You want to use the middle of the bat even for a defensive shot. Then if the ball bounces a little more than you anticipate, you have plenty of bat left with which to make contact. Play with your hands too near the ground and any ball with extra lift is likely to hit the splice or your glove and give the possibility of a catch.

It is absolutely vital that your top hand keeps in control throughout this shot. If it does not, you will not be able to achieve a slightly angled bat at the completion of the shot. You will readily appreciate the problems of a bat angled upward as the bottom hand pushes through, so keep control in the top hand so that the ball goes from a bat angled to play it down.

As mentioned earlier, the forward defensive shot is used to counter the most dangerous ball you have to face—straight, on

Problems which so often appear in the forward defensive.
1. The bottom hand has pushed through to offer a catch to slip as the bat face turns.
2. The batsman has planted his front foot down the wrong line.

The batsman has been bowled because he has gone on to the wrong line with a dominant bottom hand closing the face of the bat as he plays across.

a good length, and possibly with lateral movement—so it is important to get the basic elements correct:

1. The bat comes down straight from a high backlift.
2. It is the head and front shoulder that lead your weight out on to the line of the ball and never the front foot leading the way.
3. The front foot takes up a natural position pointing towards extra-cover as it lands, the front knee is bent and the back leg almost straight.
4. The top hand controls the bat as it comes down close to the front pad, with the bottom hand relaxing as contact with the ball is made with a full face of the bat.
5. Stay sideways and get your head, held straight, out past your front knee.
6. Above all, wait to see line and length before committing yourself to moving forward.

THE DRIVES

Driving without due care and attention is a motoring offence. It is also an offence when batting, and the punishment for such a crime is usually a lengthy spell of confinement in the pavilion. Bad driving leads to so many dismissals, and yet batsmen have so many opportunities to score heavily from overpitched deliveries that to waste them really is a crime. In fact, it is often said that a batsman who cannot drive is only half a batsman. So, where do we go wrong when we miss out on a juicy half-volley?

The first question to be answered is—was it really a half-volley? Remember that the bowler is trying to deceive the batsman into playing a false shot anyway. So, the batsman himself must be careful to select the right ball to drive and not make the bowler's job easy. To help cover any slight error in judgement, use a full follow-through when you drive off the front foot. Against the really quick bowlers at the start of your innings you might check the follow-through because the pace of the ball on to the bat gives you all the power you require. However, when you face the spinners or medium pacers, a full swing of the bat can offer a larger margin for error. You might go for the off-drive, not quite get to the ball, but still play the shot. In those circumstances a checked swing will in all probability see the ball looping to mid-off and you are out. If you continue with the follow-through, the same circumstances might well see the ball clearing mid-off and still going to the boundary.

The actual mechanics of the shot are similar to the forward defensive. It is your head and front shoulder which lead out on to the line of the delivery and you keep sideways-on as the bat comes straight down from a high backlift. The difference is that once you have spotted that the ball is over pitched, there is more acceleration of the bat into the hitting zone. This continues, with the arms extending so that the hands are 'thrown' in the direction in which the ball has been struck. As you swing right through, the wrists do not break until the arms have been fully extended. The bat finishes over your front shoulder with the top hand still gripping tightly. If the hands have been used correctly, the bat handle will be pointing in the direction the ball has travelled at the completion of the shot. If you have checked the swing, it is the blade itself which points after the ball. In the same way as when you check the swing in the forcing shot off the back foot, the bat becomes an extension of the top forearm, with that top hand still firmly in control.

One of the biggest mistakes in driving is to allow your head to come up as you hit the ball. This allows the bottom hand to come into the shot early and you will end up hitting across the line, shutting the face of the bat and ruining the timing of the shot as the ball comes off the toe rather than the middle. The rule is to stay down and maintain the shape right through the shot. As well as keeping your head down, you must also guard against letting it fall away to the off-side. This was important to a successful forward defensive: it represents a major disaster area in the drive. It tends to become particularly evident when driving from middle and leg or leg stump towards mid-on. Keep your eyes parallel to the ground at all times. In the same way, make sure that you keep a good shape by preventing the back foot from pivoting. If it does, the hips and shoulders turn and it is unlikely that you will be able to throw those hands right through in the direction of the ball.

Problems can also occur if you try to drive inside out. Instead of hitting across the line from off to leg as the bottom hand comes in as you either pivot or fall to the off, in this case you

A superb straight drive with the batsman just leaning into the ball from a quicker bowler.
1. The shape is right, with the head in advance of the front knee.
2. The top hand is still in control with the bat face absolutely square to the delivery and now pointing straight after the ball.
3. There has been good extension of the bottom arm through the line of the ball.
4. The back leg is only slightly flexed.
5. The back foot is parallel to the crease although the heel has been allowed to rise off the ground.

A splendid example of the off-drive.
1. The batsman has stayed down in the shot, not allowing his head to come up.
2. He has extended his arms through the ball, with the bat handle now pointing to where the ball has gone.
3. He created a firm base by pointing his front foot towards extra-cover.

This is a wipe across the line rather than an on-drive through it.
1. The head has started to fall away to the off.
2. The right hand has come in to close the face of the bat.
3. The back foot has pivoted.

Yorked!
1. The head has fallen right over to the off-side.
2. The bottom hand has pushed horribly across the line.

The on-drive, with a full swing of the bat against a slow bowler.
1. The batsman's head has not fallen over towards the off-side, as so often happens.
2. His front foot is not too straight and has landed in the correct position because the head has led out to the ball.

Playing this on-drive, the batsman has not over-stretched with his front foot. He has let the ball come up to him.

The left-hander has driven at a wide ball and given a catch to slip.
1. He has stayed bolt upright, making no effort to lead into the shot with his head and front shoulder.
2. The open face of the bat is a long way from his body.

Bowled through the gate. Early commitment of the front foot has meant it landed in the wrong place and too straight. This has resulted in balance problems and the late adjustment, hitting inside out, is to no avail.

Moving out to drive, the batsman has kept sideways-on as he went to the pitch of the ball and followed right through. As he is hitting over the top rather than along the ground, there is a marked difference to the trunk position illustrated.

The lofted straight drive.
1. The trunk and head have come up, but the head has remained nicely upright for balance and poise.
2. The shot has been played with a full arm extension as the bat is allowed to flow freely through.

are hitting across the line from leg to off. Thus, a ball on leg stump is driven through the off-side. Except that it is not really a drive so much as a push, as the bottom hand once again comes into play to ruin the timing. Furthermore, as you push out towards the off you are liable to leave a nasty gap between bat and pad, and there is every chance that a ball coming back towards the stumps off the pitch will get through.

When you have the shot grooved to your satisfaction, you can expand your repertoire by moving down the pitch to drive. In this way you are looking to turn a good length ball from a slow bowler into a half-volley. The important thing here is to maintain a sideways shape as you move out to meet the ball. You can keep sideways by bringing the back foot up behind or to the front foot after your head has led an initial front foot movement. Never let your head bob up and down as you make ground to the ball. You should glide out as if on runners. When you have arrived close to the pitch of the ball, you then apply the same principles that you did when driving from the crease. These are:

1. Stand still until you are sure that the ball is there to be driven from a high backlift.
2. Keep sideways-on with your head straight, and lead out on to the line of the ball with your head and front shoulder.
3. Your front foot will automatically go to the right spot. Have the toes of this foot pointing into the covers, take up your weight on a bent front leg, with the back leg almost straight and never pivoting.
4. Keep down in the shot as you hit through the ball with a full arm extension and with the top hand in control throughout.

These principles apply when you are aiming to stroke the ball along the ground. However, there will be times when you want to loft the ball over the straight fielders' or bowler's head. This might sound highly adventurous, but provided there are no fielders stationed at long-on or long-off, it should be safe enough to loft the ball into the vacant areas. Obviously you should not attempt to do so until well set.

We have already established that when we want to keep the ball along the ground we have to drive with the front foot close to the pitch of the ball. When aiming over the top you do not want to be quite as close. This applies whether you are driving from the crease or advancing down the pitch, as is often the case when your intention is to hit a six. There is no point in playing this shot unless you are going for a six. This means that you have to go right through with the shot, so a full follow-through of the bat is essential.

Remember that you are trying to hit the ball straight, so pay attention to keeping a sideways shape with the top hand totally in control. If you open up and allow the bottom hand to take charge, your straight drive will become an ungainly slog to cow shot corner. Beware of leaning back too far and lifting your head in anticipation of where the ball is going. Do this and it will not go very far, for all the timing will disappear. You can come up in the shot a little, but only as contact is made and never before.

THE GLANCE

There are two ways of dealing with a ball of full length going down the leg-side. You must make sure that both are missing leg stump or the only glance that will interest you is likely to be a quick one in the umpire's direction as he gives you out! The half-volley can be clipped away between square leg and long leg, while if the delivery is of full length, but not a half-volley, you can come forward and glance the ball into the arc between

The safe way to play the leg glance off the front foot.
1. The batsman has led on to the line of the ball with his head.
2. The top hand is in control as the face of the bat begins to shut.

This batsman is in all sorts of trouble as he tries to glance a ball which is too straight for the shot.
1. His head is falling away.
2. The bottom hand is pushing through, resulting in a catch to backward short leg.

square leg and fine leg. In both cases we are talking about facing bowling mainly of medium pace or above. You need the pace of the ball coming on to the bat. This is a delicate shot and you are not adding any momentum to the ball.

The clip is a variety of the glance played so that should you miss it, the ball strikes your front pad. You cannot swing through the pad, which, as you are playing round it and across the line of the ball, is why you only play the shot when the ball is certain to miss leg stump. It is a shot played from directly under your nose, so you have to let the ball come right up to you and make certain that you do not allow your head to topple over towards the off-side. If you do, you will find the face of the bat shutting too early and you will lack the timing so essential to playing it successfully. You do not need to let the bottom hand shut the face in the hitting zone, but only as contact is made.

If the ball is overpitched, but not a half-volley down the leg-side, you can lead forward with your head and front shoulder as you would for the forward defensive. However, instead of playing the ball with the full face of the bat, as you would in defence, you can just close the face to deflect the ball away for runs. It is quite safe to do so, for it is a pre-condition that the ball should be missing the stumps. You can, however, play the glance to a straighter delivery than you would attempt to clip, so you have to be doubly certain that the ball is not going to straighten on pitching. This means that although it appears to be missing in the air, when it hits the pitch it comes back towards the stumps.

You need a certain feel in the hands to play this shot, and that only comes from being able to control the bat with your hands working together. The top hand is in command, but once again the bottom hand is allowed to close the face as contact is made. If this happens too early you will have problems, as you will if you commit yourself on to the wrong line or if you allow your head to fall away. You have to be patient, choose the right line and let the ball come right up to you. Whereas when you clip the ball away you are hitting it, with the glance it is a case of letting the ball hit the bat.

A well-controlled sweep.
1. The head has led the forward movement on to the line of the ball, and has not turned.
2. The ball has been correctly hit at a full arm's stretch.
3. The weight is completely on the front foot.
4. The back knee has sunk to the ground.

The most common problems associated with the sweep.
1. The head has turned in the intended direction of the shot before the point of contact.
2. There is no arm extension and the bottom hand has taken over.
3. Early commitment means that the front foot has gone on to the wrong line.

THE SWEEP

As was said earlier, the glances are generally played against the medium pacers and above. Against a spinner who bowls a good length on a pitch not offering high bounce but who strays outside the leg stump, you can employ the sweep. If there is high bounce in the pitch there is every possibility that you will get a top edge, while if the ball is too full you might well be yorked as the cross bat swings over it.

As with all cross-batted shots, indeed as with all shots, you want a high backlift so that you are coming down on to the ball. Once again it is your head that leads out on to the line of the ball, with your weight being taken up on a bent front leg. Your head must lead the leg out on to the right line so that the ball will always hit the pad if you miss it. If a spinner brings the ball back into the stumps from outside leg, you cannot be lbw, so that pad is a total safeguard against getting bowled. Contact is made with the bat as horizontal as possible and as near a full arm's stretch as possible, even if this cannot always be achieved. Keep watching for unpredictable bounce, so do not turn your head until after contact has been made and the shot completed. As you do make contact, the back leg can be allowed to sink to the ground, but if this happens too early you will be getting underneath the ball and lobbing catches to square leg. The arc between square leg and mid-wicket is the target area, for provided you have got into the correct position, you will not be able to sweep towards fine leg. As contact is made, the wrists are allowed to roll a little just to make sure you are helping the ball downward.

The sweep has often been labelled a dangerous shot. It can be, but not if played properly. Misjudgement of line is perhaps the most common reason for a disaster. If you try to sweep a ball pitching in line with the stumps, you might well be trapped lbw. If you allow your head to fall away, you will find it that much more difficult to judge the right line. You might well then put your front foot outside the line, miss the ball, and get bowled. If you do not play the ball at a full arm's stretch you are likely to mishit it, if you make any contact at all, while allowing the bottom hand to come in too early inevitably leads to a lofted shot.

Played with technique and judgement, the sweep is both safe and profitable, so make certain you follow the rules:

1. After the high backlift the head and front shoulder lead onto the line and does not turn until the shot has been completed.
2. The front leg takes up your weight and the back leg is allowed to sink as contact is made. If you miss, the ball always hits the front pad.
3. You aim to make contact at a full arm's stretch, rolling the wrists to help the ball down towards the gap between square leg and mid-wicket.

BOWLING

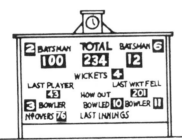

PREPARING TO BOWL

It is possible simply to take the ball from the skipper, measure out a run and bowl. However, it is not possible to be at your most effective without proper preparation. No matter whether you are going to bowl at the start of play or well into the innings, there is usually a relationship between how well you bowl and how well you have warmed up.

Before the start of a match it is a good idea to do your preparation on the edge of square. All the bowlers, and not only the openers, can do this. Put in some stumps so that there is a target at which to bowl and go through a programme of acclimatization to the day's conditions. Presuming that you align the stumps with the pitch on which you are going to play, and that you have a bowl from both ends, you will discover the influence of wind conditions, what length you need to bowl to hit the top of the stumps with a straight ball, and at which end you feel more comfortable. This last point is an important one. Bowlers tend to be temperamental characters. If a bowler thinks he likes the pavilion end rather than going downhill and downwind from the gasworks end, the chances are he will bowl better from the pavilion end. Captains should be aware of this and, wherever possible, accommodate such foibles.

It is a serious mistake not to go through some warm-up exercise before bowling, so that you are loose and supple. There is less likelihood of strains and pulls if you get warm before you perform the highly complex and rigorous physical action that is bowling. Once you have got supple and mobile, you can aim for that essential rhythm by bowling at least one over off your full run before play begins. If you don't open the bowling make sure you get an early warning from the captain before you start your spell, so that you can get properly warmed up while in the field.

It is important to be ready to bowl with full effect from the very first ball you send down. Too many bowlers use their first two or three overs to get warmed up, and by that time the batsmen have had a chance to get their eye in. Never provide the batsmen with a few gentle sighters that do not really test them. Opening bowlers especially should be prepared to bowl at top speed right from the outset. After all, that is when the batsmen are at their most vulnerable and when the ball is in the best condition.

Medium pacers will hope to swing the ball from the outset, but in the first two or three overs line and length will be more important than lateral movement. The great medium pacers have always been renowned for accuracy in their opening overs. While giving nothing to the batsmen, they are all the time exploring conditions to find the best way to achieve swing or movement off the seam that day. If that movement comes early, it is a bonus. Similarly with the spinners, it is a gradual process rather than going for significant turn immediately.

Once line and length have been achieved, it should not take too much adjustment to the basics to find some lateral movement, be it swing or spin. Your own physical behaviour will have to be taken into account. Good bowlers of whatever type will have an acute bodily awareness. They will know that, for some reason, their arm is a bit lower than it was yesterday, their wrist is not snapping into the action as usual, or perhaps they are not getting absolutely sideways-on in the delivery. Going through a mental checklist to be aware of things like that enables them to correct the faults immediately or, at least, compensate for them on a temporary basis.

ASSESSING THE BATSMAN

Given that you should be attempting to bowl consistently on a good line and length, you should continually be looking at the batsmen to assess their strengths and weakenesses in order to know exactly what that good line and length is. A ball of full length to the average batsman on or just outside off stump can become cannon fodder to the 6 foot 6 inch man who can only play the drive. So consider what you are up against before choosing the line and length of your attack. Does the batsman favour the front or back foot? Does he open or shut the face as he plays? Is he predominantly an off- or on-side player? Once you know these things you have a much clearer picture of what to bowl at him, and consequently how to set your field.

Study the stance and grip very closely. This can give you a clue to what type of batsman he is before he even hits a ball. As a general rule, a batsman who grips the bat low down or with his hands well apart on the bat handle is more likely to be a pusher and deflector or a puller and cutter rather than a flowing driver of the half-volley. It is not a concrete rule, for you might well pitch it right up to such a player, expecting the ball to be pushed gently into the covers, only to find it winging into the next parish. Cricket can be an infuriating game like that! Similarly, as a general rule, when bowling to the batsman whose head is hanging over to the off-side in his stance, you should aim for a middle and leg or leg stump line. Ninety per cent of the time such a batsman's balance will fall away to the off as soon as he moves, so the ball on the leg stump will have him playing across the line. A good grip and a sideways stance could well indicate a batsman strong on the off-side, while an open stance and a bottom hand creeping round the back of the handle might suggest preference for the on-side. If the backlift goes out towards third man, consider bowling an away-swinger at off stump or just outside. Unless he adjusts in the hitting zone, this type of batsman is likely to get into trouble against such a delivery as the face of the bat will close as he brings it down. However, if the pick-up goes towards fine leg, there is every chance he will tend to play inside out and so be susceptible to an inswinger.

MEDIUM AND FAST-MEDIUM BOWLING

Traditionally the most successful bowler in English cricket has been the fast-medium type. He gets assistance from the green pitches and will have the ability to swing the ball in the air. This being the case, it is a great pity not to look after the tool of your trade—the ball—if you are this type of bowler. You should keep it in the best possible condition to achieve lateral movement through the air.

It is an awful waste, in conditions that favour the medium pacer, if he allows the ball to get into poor condition. The seam, especially, should be kept clean. It is illegal to raise the seam, but you are allowed to pick out any pieces of dirt of mud. You should always ensure that one side is kept well polished. Agree with the bowler at the other end which side is to be polished and work hard on it. Most bowlers accept that the side with the lesser amount of lettering or design is the one which keeps its shine longer, so take every opportunity to buff-up that side. Most teams will have a particularly good polisher in its midst, and at the fall of a wicket or the end of an over let him have a go at working up the shine.

Even an old ball can be encouraged to swing. Some bowlers use saliva to get one side of the ball very wet. Putting that side on the outside of the intended curve can get appreciable swing even with an old ball. Apparently the moisture forms a smooth surface over which the air passes more quickly than the untreated side, thus favouring lateral movement towards the dry side. It all sounds like data from wind tunnel tests on a guided missile, but the rough and shiny sides of the ball work on exactly the same principles. It does not matter if you don't understand the higher physics involved, just that you know what happens when you take hold of the ball in a certain way.

If you bowl at medium pace or above and are unsure which way you should be trying to swing the ball, your basic action should give you a clue. If you get sideways-on as you bowl, you should stand more chance of swinging the ball away from the right-handed batsman. If you land rather open at the crease, there is a better possibility that you will be an inswing bowler. A video recording will tell you into which category you fall or, failing that, ask a colleague to watch you bowl.

The video or your colleague will also be able to give you an idea as to what you should be trying to bowl by focusing in on your hand as you release the ball. The hand position, more than anything else, can determine the way the ball should swing. If your hand and fingers remain behind the ball at the moment of release, you sound like a natural outswinger. If your hand and fingers cut down the off-side of the ball as you let it go, it is almost certain that you will find it easier to bowl inswingers.

In either case you will want to grip the ball with two fingers on top of the seam and the thumb supporting it underneath. This will help you get the necessary whipped backspin which will help keep the ball on an even keel aerodynamically.

The grip for the outswinger. The seam rests on the side of the thumb and points towards the slips while held vertical. The shinier side of the ball is to the on-side of the pitch.

The grip for the inswinger. The seam rests on the flat of the thumb and points towards leg slip. The shinier side is to the off. The first and second fingers are slightly closer together on top of the ball than for the outswinger.

Perhaps rudder would be a better nautical analogy than keel, for it is the upright seam going through the air that helps it to swing. If you are looking to make it swing away, grip the ball with the side of the thumb under the seam, which should be pointing towards the slips. Get sideways-on as you deliver the ball and follow through with the bowling arm chasing the front arm right over and across the body to finish outside the front thigh. The inswing bowler does not need to get quite so sideways-on, and the bowling arm, as a general rule, finishes on or just inside the front thigh. In this case the ball is held with

A side view of a perfectly acceptable inswing action.
1. He is about to use his front arm, even if the chest-on approach does not allow him to get the arm quite as far back as with a sideways action.
2. The bowler keeps his head upright as he looks inside the front arm.
3. The front leg has come up to help him lean back.
4. The right foot has landed parallel to the crease.

the seam on the flat of the thumb and pointing towards leg slip.

Having got hold of the ball in the correct manner, you need to run up to the wicket to bowl. As a rule you want to deliver the ball from close to the stumps so that your arm is going over between wicket and wicket. In this way you are aiming straight at the stumps at the other end at the outset of your delivery and still leaving the major wicket-taking opportunities—bowled, caught and lbw—open to you. If you bowl from wide of the crease as a right-arm bowler going over the wicket to a right-handed batsman, you are cutting down on those opportunities. From wide of the crease, the straight ball hitting the stumps will not be on a line between wicket and wicket until it is three yards from the batsman's stumps. It is therefore simple for the batsman to get his pad outside the line of the off stump and, if playing a shot, he cannot then be lbw. If he gets into that position, you are not going to bowl him, so the chances of taking a wicket are drastically reduced. Furthermore, if you deliver from wide of the crease you have to be aiming towards the leg-side merely to bowl a straight ball. If your arm is coming over close to the stumps, however, the angle the straight ball travels is not going towards the danger zone.

Having established, therefore, that it is definitely to the bowler's advantage to deliver from close to the stumps, the run-up should be slightly angled. This will help you to get in tight to the wicket and prevents you from falling away too quickly. The right-arm bowler then takes off from his left foot as it lands immediately prior to the delivery. He jumps high enough to get in his body turn so that he lands in a sideways position. If the jump is too high, he loses his forward momentum; too low and he is not in the air long enough to turn sideways.

Questions are often asked as to how long a run should be. There is no hard and fast answer because each bowler is an individual with different factors determining the length of run needed. The bowler's bulk and athleticism affects the distance he needs to run to the wicket before comfortably reaching optimum speed. To establish the length of run you need, run away from the stumps and put down a marker roughly at the point you feel you want to bowl. Then fine-tune the run by going back towards the stumps until your feet are falling in the right spot every time. Measure the distance in paces between the bowling crease and the adjusted mark, and you then know exactly the distance of your run. You can pace it out anywhere in the world and know that you are going to arrive at exactly the spot to deliver the ball.

You should have an even stride pattern as you run in, gathering momentum until you reach the stumps. To pick up this smooth approach, lean forward just a little and keep your head still. No bowler who bowls with the control sought by every medium pacer comes to the crease with his head bobbing up and down all along his run. Having said that, you should lean forward in your run and never look down at the ground after you have hit your marker. For the first few strides, either walking or running slowly, you can look at your mark to ensure that you start the business part of your run with the same foot hitting the same point every time. From then on, however, you run in looking at the target, not your feet. Keep

A medium pace bowler at the start of his delivery.
1. The head is held beautifully straight all through the action.
2. The front arm is just about to be thrown up and back.
3. The body is already beginning to turn into a sideways position.
4. The bowler is pushing off from his left foot into the bound.

The bound.
1. The front arm has gone up and back.
2. The bowler looks behind the front arm by arching his back, but keeping his head upright.
3. His right foot is still some inches off the ground as he jumps high enough to get into a sideways position for delivery.

Maintaining his basic position, the bowler is about to deliver the ball. The high front leg has helped rock him back and get body into the action. The right foot could perhaps be a little more parallel to the crease to ensure he remains sideways-on throughout the action.

The front foot has landed, the front arm begins to pull down through the target, while the bowling arm has commenced its swing round.

The point of release.
1. The bowling arm has swung round to release the ball as it passes the ear.
2. The head is still fixed on the target.
3. The front arm is pulling through close to the front thigh.
4. The front foot has naturally landed pointing towards fine leg to keep balance as the bowler's weight goes over the top of his front leg.

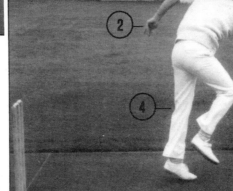

Immediately after release.
1. The head is following through towards the target.
2. The front arm is swinging back on its way to a more or less vertical position.
3. The bowling arm chases the front arm close to the front thigh.
4. The left leg, having been slightly flexed, straightens to push the bowler into his follow-through.

The batsman's view of a bowler about to deliver the ball. As the bowler turns sideways in his bound, he will look at the target from behind his raised front arm.

The perfect follow-through.
1. The front arm has pulled right back and is now almost vertical. It has remained swinging along the target line the whole way.
2. The bowler's head is still upright and he has watched the target throughout his action.
3. The bowling arm has chased the front arm right through to finish well past the body.

From this position the bowler has no chance of turning sideways so that his front shoulder and hip lead into the action. He will be chest-on as he delivers.

looking at the target from that point, through the action and into the follow-through. A surprising number of bowlers have no idea what they look at when they run in to bowl. Some will say they look at the batsman, some the stumps, but few state honestly and categorically what they look at. In a sport which involves aiming at a target, such as darts or archery, the player looks at the point where he wants his dart or arrow to land throughout the exercise. Bowling is no different, so keep your eyes fixed on the spot where you want the ball to pitch.

You will only be able to achieve this if you have a good, smooth run-up. If you lack balance on the approach, your head starts to wobble and it will be impossible to keep looking at the target. Overstriding is probably the most common cause of lost balance. Gather momentum smoothly without striving for extra pace or taking extra long paces. The key word governing the approach to the wicket is rhythm. Lose rhythm and loss of control cannot be far away.

Once you have gathered momentum and reach the point of delivery, everything should be positioned to get first yourself and then the ball travelling down the selected line. If you are

In this instance the bowler is failing to get properly off the ground as he bounds into his delivery stride. In fact, he is hardly bounding at all, being close to the ground and so finding it difficult to get sideways.

bowling at off stump, imagine a line drawn from the base of that stump going through the point from which you are about to deliver the ball, and continuing back past you. Your run will have brought you in at a slight angle to this line, as already discussed. However, from the point when you join the imaginary line, all your momentum is channelled down it.

As you jump, your front shoulder turns so that your front arm is thrown straight, with the head still looking at the target from over the shoulder. As the back foot lands parallel to the bowling crease, the front arm, which had been thrown up and back away from the batsman, is pulled down sharply, with the little finger edge of the hand extended down the target line. As the front arm is driven back close to the front thigh, the bowling arm comes over. This hand turns out so that the thumb leads the way back down the arc of delivery. This movement is important as it ensures that, as the arm begins to

This left-arm bowler has failed to use his front arm despite the fact that he has attempted to lean back as he delivers.

come up and over, the fingers have got into a position right behind the ball. In effect, the wrist is now cocked, with the inside of the wrist leading the way over for as long as possible before snapping through at the release. After the release, the arm continues through to finish well past the outside of the front thigh.

What is happening to the feet and legs while all this is going on up above? In fact, the front leg lands in a slightly bent position, or gives a little at the knee as it lands with the front foot just across the pitch. As the ball is released, the front leg straightens. If the front shoulder has done its work, the feet should follow down the target line, while the pull of the arms when working well catapults the body forward down the same line as the front leg straightens. The back leg comes through close to the front leg. If it flails out, the chances are that balance has been lost; it is either compensating for a falling

Apart from the fact that he is about to deliver a no ball, the bowler is taking such a long delivery stride that he will find it virtually impossible to get his weight over the top of the front leg.

head or the head will fall away to balance the wide leg action. The result is likely to be the same in either case. As the bowler falls to the off he fires the ball down the leg-side. If you suffer from frequently bowling down the leg, check that your entire action is moving down the target line and not falling away.

It is only in the follow-through that the natural pull of the arm movement drags you out on the off-side away from the pitch. Even so, strive to keep to your head moving down the target line for as long as possible. Just as in batting, the head is the key to good bowling. Keep it upright and moving down the target line and you have the basis for a sound action. You need to be aware of what your head is doing right through the

Instead of the front arm pulling through close to the front thigh, the bowler is allowing his arm to splay out. The bowling arm follows in the same plane and so accuracy is likely to be inconsistent.

delivery, just as you need to be aware of what is happening to all parts of your body. Then, when things do not go quite as you want, you should be able to isolate different facets of the action in your mind to pinpoint the fault. Once you realize, for example, that you are not landing with your back foot parallel to the crease or you are not turning as you jump, you can correct the fault.

The great virtue of the medium pacer is that he can achieve a high level of consistency. However, he will want to have some variations to his standard delivery, all the while concealing them so that they appear as a normal ball. He might deliver from close to the stumps in the prescribed manner most of the

This bowler's head has fallen away as he delivers and he is therefore unlikely to bowl as consistently straight as a bowler who keeps his head upright as he bowls.

time, yet just occasionally bowl from wide of the crease or just a little wider than usual. All the time he will be aiming to pitch the ball in the same place so that he induces the same shot to a ball which is on a different line. If this has been tried and yet the batsman is still there, a different ploy can be attempted. If you suspect that the batsman is reading your intentions, go wide of the crease but deliver the ball from a lower arm. Now it

If this bowler should deliver a good ball, he is unlikely to know. His head has fallen to look at the ground in front of him rather than the target, and his front leg is far too bent.

will look as if you are on the wide line, but in fact your arm is coming over from the same place as when you bowl close to the stumps.

Variation of pace is another weapon of the medium pacer. Again, maintaining line and length is the priority or the ruse will be quickly identified. For instance, the slower ball must be bowled to a full length. The intention is to get the batsman driving at the ball which is not quite there, so that he offers a catch to mid-on or mid-off. Alternatively, a succession of balls held back just a little can be followed by a delivery at top pace. Such a tactic can often induce the batsman to play late. In either case you should never give the batsman a warning that a different delivery is coming. Even with the slower ball, do not change your action to reduce pace. It is far better just to put the ball further back into your hand rather than holding it in the

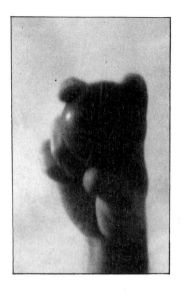

Most frequently bowled by the outswing bowler, the off-cutter uses a similar grip. The fingers on top of the ball are spaced a little wider, and the index finger will pull down on the leg-side as the ball is released.

Again, the fingers are spaced a little wider on top of the ball compared with the inswing grip. To bowl the leg-cutter, the second finger is dragged down the off-side to the ball on release.

fingers, and go right through with your action in the normal way. Obviously the place to practise such strategies is in the nets. You will invariably get it wrong if you try to introduce them in the course of a match. It takes time and effort to master a slower ball or a yorker, so work at it in the nets to ensure it is a honed skill when you apply it in the middle.

Cutters are another means of introducing some variety into the swing bowler's armoury. Again, problems can arise if you decide to go out in a match one day and try bowling a cutter. Practise in the nets first. In general, the away-swing bowler will find it easier to bowl an off-cutter, while the inswinger should be more naturally suited to the leg-cutter. Very simply, this is because the outswing bowler is used to keeping his fingers behind the ball as he bowls, so it is not asking very much more just to drag the index finger down the leg-side of the ball as it is released. Combined with a movement of the hand down that side of the ball and underneath as it is released, and the ball will cut back from the off-side towards the leg. Conversely, the leg-cutter is bowled by dragging the middle finger down the off-side of the ball on release while the wrist turns in towards the body. This gets the ball moving from leg to off on pitching and requires only a slight adjustment from the inswing bowler's usual hand action.

Whether you are aiming to bowl a leg-cutter or an off-cutter, it is important to keep the ball well pitched up. The object is to get the batsman playing forward because he then has less time to adjust to any movement you might achieve. If you drop the ball short, the batsman will merely go back and play the movement as he sees the ball leave the pitch.

FAST BOWLING

There has never been a lack of medium pace bowlers in English cricket. At all levels there are good bowlers able to use typical English conditions well. What is generally lacking is the genuine quickie capable of beating good batsmen by sheer pace. There are several reasons for this. In general, English pitches do not themselves offer pace and bounce to a bowler. There seems little point in investing the physical effort required if the end result is a fast ball through the air which 'dies' on pitching, but the potential rewards make it all worthwhile in the end. Fast bowling is hard work and anyone embarking on a career as a quick bowler needs encouragement. Given the choice between straining every fibre or gently running in and turning your arm over for the same reward, not many bowlers take the more demanding option.

Perhaps because conditions do not really favour genuinely fast bowlers, there are few models to which young bowlers can aspire and so they become rarer. Also, it is true to say that coaches cannot necessarily handle the promising young fast bowler. They tend to ask him to slow down, master line and length, and then try to bowl fast. When the young bowler cuts down his pace he may or may not gain control of line and length. Whether he does or not, he is unlikely to go back to bowling quickly if he gets similar success for less effort. In the West Indies, for instance, quick bowlers are encouraged to bowl quicker and the odd loose delivery is tolerated in the knowledge that for every five wayward deliveries there might be one unplayable straight one. The objective then is to improve on the ratio, not detract from the positive attributes.

So what are the requirements of a fast bowler? To begin with, he must think like a fast bowler. He must enjoy the sensation of bowling quickly. As an attacking force, he must be aggressive on the field. The notion of hating batsmen is perhaps going a little over the top when talking about aggression. Instead, he should hate the idea of batsmen being able to withstand his will to take wickets. In addition, he will need endless dedication and determination. In a word, he will need guts to succeed.

There are also obvious physical requirements. Strength is uppermost among them. It is wiry strength rather than bulky strength which is required, for the fast bowler will also need mobility and flexibility. Size can be an advantage, for you will get more bounce bringing the ball down from a considerable height. So, it is unlikely that a genuinely fast bowler will be under 5 foot 10, but at the same time, few exceed 6 foot 4. Once you get above that height it is difficult to co-ordinate all parts of the action in one explosive effort.

Very tall fast bowlers have been far and few between, and they tend to have short careers as injuries lessen their effect. Fast bowling does put wear and tear on a frame of whatever size, so physical fitness is of prime importance. If you do have the ability to bowl fast with a wiry strength, powerful legs and a broad backside, make sure you get your body into top physical condition so that it can sustain the effort asked of it.

At the sort of pace we are talking about, it is still possible to get movement through the air although such movement is often confined to the great bowler. Experiment by angling the seam to see if you can swing it, but it might be better to grip the ball with the seam pointing straight down the pitch. Then there is a possibility that you might just hit the edge of the seam and get some movement off the pitch. To bowl quickly, you need a supple wrist that gives some whip to the delivery. The ball should therefore be held in the fingers quite lightly. If you are trying to squeeze the pips out of it as you run in, your wrist will never be relaxed enough to add that essential zip to your bowling.

The actual run-up should be smooth and rhythmical. Speed comes from rhythm, and that should commence at the very start of the run. You should not have to leap too high in the delivery stride, because your momentum will keep you in the air long enough to turn sideways. You will travel further while leaping in the air but never achieve great height. The front foot will not go across the pitch but land straighter than that of the medium pacer, otherwise it will 'block' the turn of the hips. The front hip also begins to turn away earlier than in the case of the medium pacer, but everything else is still moving straight down the delivery line.

One other point about the action itself. You might be aiming to bowl quickly, but you should never rush the early stages of the action. Speed can only come from a good action, so make sure you give yourself time to use the action properly. It is a very common mistake for young bowlers who are asked to bowl fast merely to run up like a sprinter and then deliver the ball in a hopeless whirl of arms and legs. Rhythm is non-existent and speed is lacking. Instead, go for a smooth approach, use all the action to 'wind up', take aim, and finally deliver the ball down the target line in an explosion of effort.

Speed is, of course, the fast bowler's most potent weapon, but even he can introduce some variation into his bowling. Use of the crease and subtle changes of pace apply just as much to the fast bowler as to the medium pacer. Remember, the fast bowler is always attacking. He is the shock bowler, not a defensive measure. Therefore all his variations are designed to take wickets. One of the most lethal for the quick bowler is the yorker. Like most weapons in the fast bowler's armoury, it should only be used sparingly, especially as there is such a small margin for error with this delivery. Just short of yorker length and it becomes an inviting half-volley; overpitch it and there is a full toss which few batsmen will spurn. You will only be able to bowl the ball straight into the blockhole at will if you practise and practise some more. The ideal is to get the ball under the lowest point of the bat's downswing, very often with extra pace to defeat any adjustment the batsman might make.

You have a greater margin for error with the bouncer, but even that loses its potency if overdone. Obviously you want to dig it in short to get the extra bounce, but the difference between a good and bad bouncer is the line on which it is

The position of the front foot for the medium pacer as he delivers the ball. The foot points towards fine leg naturally as it lands.

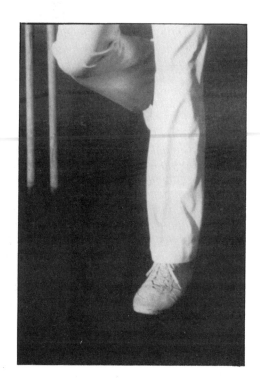

For the fast bowler, who needs to open his hips out earlier in the action, the front foot lands rather straighter than for the medium pacer.

bowled. Fire it down the leg-side and it represents an awful waste of effort. You should be aiming to deliver the ball on middle and off or middle stump so that the batsman has to get into position to play it as an initial movement. Having committed him to playing the ball, you then have a good chance of inducing a false shot and so getting a catch. Even if he does not give a catch, and the ball whistles past his throat, he should be sufficiently shaken up to grant you the ascendancy for the next ball. If you can follow the bouncer with a fast yorker, you will often find the batsman on the back foot and easy prey.

With all fast deliveries, there is no point in putting in all this effort if you are not making the batsman play. Whack it down wide and the batsman can merely watch it pass in the knowledge that you have wasted energy. The only way you will then get wickets is if the batsman makes an error. If you attack the stumps you will still pick up wickets from the batsman's errors, but you will also get them in your own right.

OFF-SPIN BOWLING

As with all styles of bowling, the off-spinner has to pay attention to his grip on the ball at the very outset. If he does not hold it properly, he will not be able to release it correctly, and without doing that he will not be able to turn it. Probably the most common mistake made by the would-be off-spinner is putting a brake on the turn. This happens when he puts his thumb on the ball. The correct grip has the thumb playing no part. Instead, there should be a good spread between the first and second fingers, with the top joint of the index finger slightly bent and on the seam. This is the part of the finger which is going to do the work of imparting spin on the ball as it leaves the hand. It is just on the inside of this top joint of the index finger that there is pressure on the ball, with the seam running under both the first and second fingers.

The idea is to ensure that the ball always pitches with the seam making contact with the ground. Being the roughest part of the ball, the seam is most likely to 'bite' and so get the ball to

The grip for the off-spinner. The thumb is kept out of the way as the first and second fingers impart the spin to the ball. The seam runs round under the top joints of these fingers.

The alternative grip for the off-break bowler. If the fingers are not long enough to get round the seam, this is a useful way to grip the ball. The index finger uses the seam as a lever as it spins the ball.

deviate off the straight. If the ball pitches on the smooth part, the friction between ball and ground is reduced and so it is less likely to spin. Therefore the idea has to be to get the ball going through the air spinning round the seam. If you imagine the ball as the world and the seam as the equator, it should travel through the air with one pole pointing at the bowler, the other

A good pre-delivery position for the off-break bowler. He has turned sideways early in his bound, he is looking at the target from behind a high front arm, and the wrist of his bowling arm is already cocked.

at the batsman and the equator always hitting the ground when it lands.

Having experimented to find out how you, as an individual bowler, need to angle the seam in your hand to achieve this every time, you are now ready to bowl. Even though you are a slow bowler, you will still need some sort of run to give you a momentum and a rhythmical approach to the crease. Usually some seven to eight yards is enough to achieve this and there is no point in going any further. As you get to the crease, gather yourself so that the front shoulder points towards fine leg. You want to get in close to the stumps, with the back foot parallel to the bowling crease.

This turn of the shoulder gives you a perfect view of the batsman from behind the front arm as you are about to bowl. It also leads the front foot to land across the pitch and pointing towards mid-wicket. You will want to take a short delivery stride, because as you release the ball there should be a

By taking a long delivery stride, the bowler cannot get over his front leg.
Consequently, he falls away to the off-side and accuracy suffers.

pronounced pivot around the front foot. You will never
achieve this if you have a long delivery stride, and without the
pivot you will not be using your body action to add to the
finger spin.

At the moment the ball is released, the index finger drags
down on the seam with the wrist turning from the off- to the
leg-side at the same time. This wrist action is always likened to
turning a door handle. Certainly it is movement in the same
direction, but it is not really the same action. The off-spinner is
combining the finger action with a turn of the wrist, all
reinforced by the body pivoting round the front leg.

When you have bowled a ball in the nets, look at the ground to see if your spikes have inscribed a circle where your front foot landed. If they have, you can be sure that you have been pivoting round that front leg. As the front foot pivots, your weight should be on the ball of this foot, even if it landed flat. As well as getting the required pivot, you also want to come up over this front foot. You will then be using your full height to gain any bounce from the pitch, and spin bowlers rely on bounce as well as turn to get their wickets. Batsmen who cope quite well with low turn will often come unstuck when the ball lifts and turns.

Coming up on to the ball of the front foot as you release the delivery also helps you to achieve a looped trajectory. This is not to be confused with a lobbed trajectory. The lobbed ball travels down a regular, predictable arc. The looped ball reaches its highest point nearer to the batsman than the bowler before descending more steeply. That is far less predictable and causes problems for the batsman who wants to assess where it is going to pitch. Similarly, a flat trajectory is not too testing, for the ball spends most of its flight below the level of the batsman's eyes. It is only when it goes above the eye-line that the batsman is asked to make serious calculations about its landing point.

As you deliver this looping off-break, remember to keep your head high and upright. Some good off-spinners talk of keeping the chin high as long as possible, others of trying to read the writing on the ball as it leaves you. Whether you use one of these little aids or not, you can check that you are keeping your head up by paying attention to your right knee. If that flays out, your head has probably fallen away. You are aiming to keep the right leg in tight to the left as you start on your follow-through. You should have a flowing follow-through rather than stopping in the action, but never collapse into it. The first two or three strides should be taken while still in an upright position before crouching to become an extra close fielder.

Even though they are slow bowlers, off-spinners sometimes show an over-eagerness to get through their action. Always give yourself time to get the full action in. This means that you must not get over that front foot too soon. It is almost a case of bowling and then stepping through rather than stepping through as you bowl. Consider that subtle difference in timing. A rushed action often occurs when you are lacking confidence or are apprehensive about bowling to a particular batsman. You want to get it over as soon as possible and so hurry

A really bad case of a lack of pivot around the front foot. There is no way that the body can reinforce the finger spin.

through. Never do so. Whatever your problems of the moment, however good the batsman you are bowling at, nothing is to be gained by letting your action go to pot. Use it all and you will bowl better.

Where is the off-spinner aiming to pitch the ball? The answer is—never short. If a spin bowler is being cut and pulled, he is not bowling well. He will not mind nearly as much if he is driven, because it is by inducing the misdrive that he is going to get wickets. So the ball is always going to be pitched up, with the direction dependent on the amount of turn offered by the pitch. If there is what might be termed normal turn, the line should be just outside off stump with the spin taking the ball on

This time the bowler has pivoted around the front foot and it has allowed him to use his whole body in the delivery.

to the stumps. If it is a flat pitch offering little encouragement to the off-spinner, he will aim at off stump, while a greater angle of turn will see him pitching wider of the off stump.

If the pitch is giving appreciable turn, the off-spinner might favour going round the wicket in order to stand more chance of getting an lbw decision. Sometimes it can be a useful variation to go round the wicket even when there is not that much turn. It just gives the batsman something else to work out and can have him playing for turn which is not there. Similarly, use the crease to add variation of line. These variations should be subtle, for a good batsman will notice if you bowl one ball from tight in to the stumps and another from the edge of the

This is a good-looking off-break action. The ball is being released from a vertical arm, the head is held high and upright, and, with a short delivery stride, the bowler is getting right over his front leg.

A common disaster for an off-spinner. The bowler has let his head drop down as he releases the ball, resulting in a flat trajectory rather than a teasing loop.

crease. If you think the batsman has noticed when you deliver from different points on the crease and is adjusting accordingly, there is another ploy to use. If you go out along the crease a little way but drop your bowling arm a little, it will look as if you are delivering from wide of the crease, but in fact the point of release will be close to the stumps. It is a pretty advanced piece of deception, but it shows what spin bowling at the highest level is all about. Remember that varying the point of release should only be an occasional exercise. The stock ball should be delivered from close to the stumps. As well as making the spin more effective, your body shields the ball for longer and does not give the batsman as long to sight it.

Such a consideration is important if you are going to employ another variation of the off-spinner—the floater or arm ball. This is a delivery which, rather than spinning into the stumps from the off-side, swings away from the right-handed batsman

A very good head position. He has held it high throughout his delivery of an off-break, but the bowler has failed to strike through with the bowling arm. There is little use of the front arm, and he has minimal pivot around the front foot.

This off-break bowler has got plenty of body into his action by really pivoting around that front foot. His front arm has followed right through and his bowling arm has chased through after it.

The grip for the arm ball, or floater. The thumb comes in to steady the ball while the index finger stays behind the seam without spinning it. The seam is held upright, slightly angled towards slip.

through the air and goes straight on towards the slips on pitching. The grip is similar to that employed by the away-swing bowler, with the index finger on top of the seam angled towards the slips and the thumb at the side of the ball to steady it. This helps to disguise the fact that it is not an off-break. To the batsman the grip looks almost identical to that used for the standard off-spinner's delivery.

Again, he will get a good idea that something special is on its way if you bowl the ball very much quicker than for the off-break. Bowl it at the same pace, but keep your hand behind the ball rather than turning the wrist, and use a full follow-through with the bowling arm finishing outside the front thigh. Do not try such a delivery in a match until you have mastered it in the nets. Even then, only use it sparingly. If it is overdone, the batsman gets used to playing it and it no longer contains the surprise element.

Rather than overdoing the floater, it is worth trying to vary the amount of spin you impart on the ball. This is particularly effective if the pitch is responsive to spin. If one ball goes a long way and the next hardly deviates off the straight, the batsman can never settle. Once again, you are dictating to him how the game is going to be played, and once you have achieved that position of superiority you are well on your way to success.

THE LEFT-ARM ORTHODOX SPINNER

The word 'orthodox' implies that this type of left-arm spinner is in some way unexciting or plain. That is not the case. It merely means that he does not bowl chinamen and googlies like the left-arm wrist spinner. He is a finger spinner bowling the mirror image of the right-arm off-spin bowler. This means that, to the right-handed batsman, he is getting the ball to spin towards the off-side.

The grip, the approach and the action are much the same as for the off-spinner except, of course, that the ball is bowled with the left hand and all the other instructions are reversed. However, the left-arm spinner will more often go round the wicket to the right-handed batsman, with an angled approach either behind the umpire or between him and the stumps. The reason for him going round the wicket is to stand a chance of an lbw decision.

In general, the left-arm spinner aims to bowl no further towards the leg-side than middle stump. Then, with the turn taking effect, the ball should straighten on to the stumps. Only if the ball is turning appreciably will he aim at middle and leg. The ball will always be pitched up because the bowler is attempting to get the batsman driving into the covers and making a mistake. Just as happens with the off-spinner, it is when driving that errors are made and wickets are taken.

Variations, too, are reminiscent of the off-break bowler. The left-arm spinner has an arm ball which is an inswinger to the right-handed batsman. When well disguised and sparingly used, it can be a powerful weapon. The batsman is looking for the ball to turn away from him but instead finds it coming in to exploit any gap which might have been left between bat and pad. Going over the wicket is another useful variation especially if the bowler has a good arm ball to come floating in

The left-arm spinner is a mirror image of the right-arm off-spinner. Bowling round the wicket, he has come between the umpire and the stumps and is delivering from a good sideways position.

to trap the batsman lbw. With the demise of leg-spin bowlers, the left-arm spinner has become an even more valuable member of a well-balanced attack in that he takes the ball away from the right-handed batsman and so provides a welcome variation to the off-spinner.

LEG-SPIN BOWLING

One of the main reasons why leg-spinners do not succeed is that they are not prepared to work at their craft. Because wrist spinners have become an increasingly rare breed, batsmen are not used to countering their wiles. This offers the potential for great success, but because it is not easy to master the requirements of a good leg-spinner, many bowlers give up along the way and so fail to reap the rewards.

As well as perseverance, the aspiring leg-spinner needs a good deal of strength. Not the strength of the fast bowler, nor the power of the batsman who wants to hit the ball a long way. The type of strength which is required is to be found in the fingers, along with a flexibility in the wrist. Many youngsters enjoy that flexibility early in their careers but, as they grow older, it is lost and they revert to finger spin or medium pace. The strength and flexibility are needed to enjoy control, while dedication is essential if that control is to be used to full effect. Because it is the most difficult style to bowl well, leg-spin demands more practice than any other. However, if a youngster does have the ability to spin the ball this way, he must be encouraged to continue. It is a case of spinning the ball first, then mastering line and length. This can take months and years, but having decided to bowl leg-spin, there are some firm guidelines to be followed.

Beginning as always with the grip, the ball should be embedded in the hand in such a way that it is firmly cradled by the first three fingers. The top joints of the index and middle finger go on the seam, while the third finger—the vital digit—is bent so that it rests alongside the seam. This is the main spinning finger. It straightens as you release the ball, while at the same time the wrist is uncocked in an anti-clockwise direction so that your hand finishes with the palm pointing towards square leg. If you do not cock the wrist, you will just roll the ball out. Then you will get little real turn. If you cock the wrist and then flip it over, you should be able to generate enough genuine spin to disconcert the batsman.

The grip for the leg-break.
The third finger runs along the seam and will impart the spin as the wrist is uncocked.

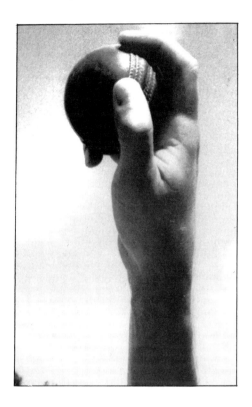

With an uncocked wrist, this leg-spinner will get virtually no spin on the ball.

As well as putting effort into flipping the wrist over and straightening that third finger, the leg-spinner must also put effort into his action. Too many bowl with an action which resembles the gentle lobbing of a hand grenade. At the end of an over you should be puffing and blowing like a medium pacer, for you should have employed as much exertion as a faster bowler. You might get away with the more flighted delivery on hard, bouncy pitches, but in England, where the surface is usually slower and lower than in the hot countries, you need to push the ball through more to inject pace into the turn.

This comes from getting a good pivot of the body into the delivery. You need an aggressive, lively approach off not too short a run. This is followed by a reasonable bound to get into a good sideways position which gives the shoulder turn and pivot to reinforce the finger and wrist action. If all three elements of the spinning action are co-ordinated, you should really get some turn. It is helped by a very positive follow-through with the bowling arm as well. Despite the fact that the leg-spinner is a slow bowler, the arm comes over quite quickly.

As the leg-spinner is in his delivery stride, his wrist is already cocked. He has got into the correct, sideways-on position and is looking behind his raised front arm.

At the moment of release, the wrist is just flicking over, while the front arm is pulling through close to the body.

A strenuous follow-through as the front arm pulls through and up, the bowling arm chases across the body, and the head follows through to the target.

It should then follow through right past the front thigh. Furthermore, it is important that it comes over through the twelve o'clock position or absolutely vertical. This will allow you to make full use of any bounce offered by the pitch and means that you get maximum value from the flip of the wrist. There can be a tendency for the bowler's head to fall away at the crucial point. This, in turn, frequently results in a poor follow-through.

It is worth considering how often words like 'aggressive' and 'positive' are used in association with leg-spin bowling. This is because the leg-spinner is an attacking bowler and should not be used in a defensive capacity. If the captain needs containment, he should turn to the medium pacers and orthodox spinners. When he wants to attack, he calls up the leg-spinner. Unless there is a very good reason to go round the wicket, the leg-spinner will always operate over in order to stand a chance of an lbw decision. The only time he will go round the wicket is to vary his line, trying to pitch in the rough outside the right-hander's leg stump.

Even when the ball is turning appreciably, you should not drift further towards the batsman's legs than middle and leg. A ball delivered over the wicket pitching leg stump will have to turn an awful lot to hit the stumps. An lbw is therefore unlikely and so there is not much reward for continually hitting the pad. You are looking to bowl at the stumps or to turn enough for the edge to the wicket-keeper, slips or gully. It is even likely that you will get a wicket from a lofted drive into the covers from an outside edge. Either way, you want the batsman on the front foot. If he goes back he will get time to watch the ball deviate off the pitch and can play accordingly. On a hard pitch with plenty of bounce there is more possibility of variable length. There the shorter ball might bounce considerably and cause the batsman problems. On typical English pitches it is necessary for the leg-spinner to nag away on a full length to cause those problems.

Within the limitations of bowling at middle and leg on a turner, or middle and off to a full length on a flat pitch, there are still variations the bowler can employ. He can deliver from close to the stumps or further along the crease, or occasionally throw the ball up and wider in the hope of inducing a poor drive. Certainly, if you are capable of bowling a googly you will want to vary the line more than if you only bowl the leg-break. If you always pitch the leg-break on middle stump and the googly outside off stump, the batsman is hardly kept guessing about the direction of turn. If you do bowl the googly, which you will need to bowl at off stump or just outside, toss in the occasional leg-break on the same line so that the googly, when it comes, will be disguised.

To bowl a googly, the point of release is when the back of the hand faces the batsman. Then, when the third finger straightens, it is imparting off-spin on the ball, although it should appear as leg-spin to the batsman. The ball, in fact, comes out of the hand over the third and little fingers. Again, to achieve this, the bowling arm must come over twelve o'clock high. The front shoulder can be allowed to drop ever so slightly if it helps you to get the release right, but avoid opening up into a chest-on position. Keep sideways. The bowling arm can then follow through straighter down the pitch without completing the swing across the front thigh as with the leg-break.

Another variation in the leg-spinner's armoury is the top-spinner. In this instance the flip of the wrist takes place a little

This leg-spinner is unlikely to turn the ball very much. His wrist is not cocked and he has failed totally to get sideways-on in his delivery.

earlier than for the leg-break, causing the spin to be straight down the line of the trajectory. The idea is to keep it pitched up but bowled a little flatter. This can get the batsman on to the back foot to a ball which he should have gone forward to, so it gathers pace off the pitch, going straight on to bowl him or trap

This bowler has a good braced front leg, but he has allowed his head to fall away to the off rather than following through down the pitch.

him lbw. The top-spinner is bowled with the back of the hand facing mid-off and the little finger directly above the thumb. Then, as the third finger straightens, the spin is all directed towards the batsman, with the bowling arm following through straight down the pitch.

As with all variations, the googly and top-spinner should be

The grip for the googly. Because the back of the hand has been turned right round towards the batsman, the spin imparted by the third finger will rotate from off to leg.

With the ball released with the seam, and therefore the spin, going straight down the pitch, the result will be a top-spinner.

used sparingly. Over-exposure will give the batsman more opportunity to read your intentions and to practise at dealing with the result. It is also important that you do not try to introduce a googly until you have the leg-break thoroughly mastered. Until that time you are likely to offer enough variation in your bowling without doing so deliberately.

WICKET-KEEPING

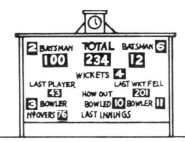

Wicket-keepers are born, not made. How many times have you heard that said? Firm guidelines are offered for every other aspect of the game, yet wicket-keepers are virtually told to go away and do their own thing. If it is successful, all well and good. If not, hard luck! Why is it that such a vital member of the side should not have the same attention paid to his technique as batsmen and bowlers? Wicket-keeping involves considerable individual application of certain basic skills. However, mistakes are not born, they are made. If a high percentage of those mistakes can be eliminated from a wicket-keeper's play, he will become a better cricketer and enjoy his game that much more. Without mistakes, the ordinary keeper can become rather useful and the good keeper outstanding.

There are three elements which are evident in the play of all good wicket-keepers. These are—in no particular order of importance—concentration, enthusiasm and positioning.

Concentration is a word that is often bandied about in cricket, but for the wicket-keeper it is more than just a word. It has to become a way of playing the game. You can often compare two keepers and note that both move well, both have safe hands. Either one is capable of pulling off the spectacular catch, and yet one is better than the other. Why? It is because he has the higher level of concentration and can maintain it throughout the session, throughout the day or throughout the match. As soon as thoughts wander away from the job in hand, concentration has gone and the standard of keeping drops.

Probably every wicket-keeper has seen a batsman crack a ball through the covers and felt just a little relieved. He is aware that he was not concentrating fully at that moment and knows just how lucky he has been. Had the ball found the edge, his lack of concentration might well have cost a valuable wicket, for he would not have reacted in time to accept the chance.

With the best keepers, such lapses are rare and will not happen more than once or twice in a career. Lower down the scale, where concentration comes and goes, the keeper can often be caught out rather than the batsman!

Concentrate on every delivery, giving it your undivided attention. There is no substitute for believing that every ball is going to come through to you. The batsman might have played the last ten overs with supreme confidence while the bowler has not once beaten the bat. Even then—especially then—you must expect the next ball to be the one which does get through, and be ready for it.

It is hard to imagine any great wicket-keeper who has not had bags of enthusiasm. It is the wicket-keeper who reflects the whole team's spirit in the field and magnifies it. It is he who keeps the bowlers going when the pitch is flat and the batsmen well-set. It is he, just as much as the captain, who keeps the fielders alert and very often he will advise the captain and bowlers. The mere presence of an enthusiastic wicket-keeper is often enough to lift the morale of a flagging team. As well as a general ebullience, he should be seen moving up to the stumps, if standing back, ready to take a return after every ball is played. Very often the ball will not come back to him, but he is still available if it does.

When preparing to take a return in earnest, he should help the fielder who is about to throw by giving him a definite target. In particular, the fielder who has chased the ball towards the boundary will, as he turns to throw, see a mass of white figures moving in every direction before him: batsmen running, fielders backing up, umpires getting into position to judge a run-out. It can be very confusing. All is made clear to him, however, if the wicket-keeper is in position at the stumps with his glove held high in the air as a target. If the return is then not inch-perfect, it is the good, enthusiastic keeper who tidies-up by going to meet it and taking the return on the full. That might seem a minor consideration, but it makes the whole fielding standard appear much higher. Having set the standard, the team then strives to live up to it.

All this concentrating and going back and forth to the stumps requires a level of physical fitness which is not exceeded by any other member of the team. As well as running, he has to bend, stretch, squat and straighten up every time a ball is bowled through the innings. Such a routine demands that the keeper has worked hard to be in prime physical condition. He has to combine the stamina of the long-distance runner with the explosive power of the sprinter, and all must be allied to the suppleness and agility of a gymnast. Keeping wicket is a physically demanding role and no wicket-keeper should take the field in a serious game unless he can measure up to those demands.

Concentration, enthusiasm and fitness are vital for the wicket-keeper who aims to perform to the best of his ability; and they are allied to the scrupulous attention he pays to the technical details of his art. Positioning is crucial. But whether he is standing up to the stumps or standing back, he needs to adopt a good stance and to take the ball well. Let us consider the stance first.

The stance is the platform on which all movement is based. It is therefore important to get the stance right so that subsequent movement from it has a chance of being correct. Just as the batsman wants to keep his head still and his eyes level to give himself the best possible chance of sighting the ball, so too does the wicket-keeper. After all, it is the same ball coming towards him.

When standing up you should get down in the conventional squatting position behind the stumps. Head up and backside down is the rule. This means that you will neither make the mistake of crouching with all your weight forward so that you collapse if you take your hands off the ground, nor with your weight back on your heels. Both of these positions are unbalanced. However, if you get into the correct position with a long straight back you will find that it is easier to keep your head still and to get the good sight of the ball which is required. Some wicket-keepers prefer to have the hands on the ground between and just in front of their toes, while others prefer the hands hanging down outside their legs. If that way suits you best, carry on, but remember that the hands have got to come together at some time, so the earlier they do the less there is to change later.

The feet should be comfortably apart with, as a general guide, the left foot in line with middle and off stumps for the right-handed batsman facing a right arm over the wicket bowler. The feet should be parallel with the toes pointing straight down the pitch. Such a position should give a clear view of the approaching ball while getting as close to the stumps as possible. As a rule, the ball will be bowled at the stumps, so you should begin in that position and thus keep the movement to a minimum if the bowler delivers a straight ball. The actual position has to be adjusted to get this good view at

A good set-up for the wicket-keeper standing up to the wicket. He has a clear view of the bowler, is within reach of the stumps, and is comfortably balanced with his eyes level.

all times. For example, you will have to stand a little wider towards the right if an off-break bowler goes round the wicket, otherwise you won't be able to see the ball down its whole flight.

One area that offers plenty of opportunities for error is the positioning in relation to the stumps. When standing up, you have to be close enough to the wicket to execute a stumping from the stance position. Few batsmen will be obliging enough to wait out of their crease while you move forward to take the bails off. Of course, you are not allowed to take the ball in front of the stumps, but you should try to get as close as possible within this limitation. This is especially important when taking catches. The nearer you can get your hands to the bat's edge, the less the opportunity for the ball to deviate.

Correct positioning is just as important when standing back. Again, you want to be able to see the ball from the moment it leaves the bowler's hand. There are several factors to determine the distance you stand back. The pace of the bowler, the speed of the pitch and the bounce of the ball can all vary. Ideally, you should be taking the ball just as it begins to lose momentum somewhere above the knee and below the waist. Because you have more time to react to the ball when standing back, there is probably no need then to squat right down. If

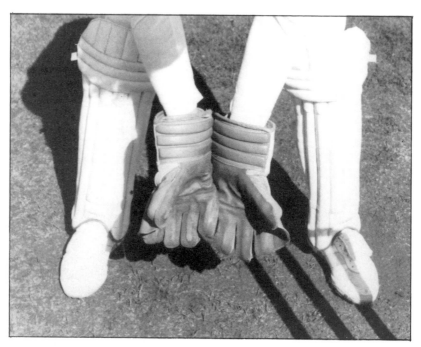

This wicket-keeper's hands are working well. His gloves are butting together right down the inside edge. Because he favours his right hand, the little finger on that hand overlaps the left as he wants to take the ball more in the right hand.

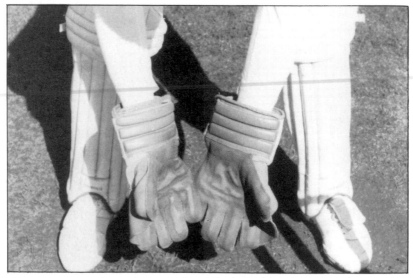

Lazy hands. Apart from the area where the little fingers overlap, the two gloves do not come together at any point. This means that there is a large area of potential weakness where the ball can pass through.

This is the view a wicket-keeper should have from his stance when standing up to the wicket. His head is just outside the line of the off stump so that he can watch the ball right through its flight.

Standing back, the wicket-keeper still wants to have a clear view of the bowler. He needs to be balanced, and he wants to keep his head still and eyes level. However, when standing back, he might prefer to take up this crouching stance rather than going right down into the more usual squatting position.

Taking the ball outside
off stump.
1. His head is right behind the ball as he takes it.
2. His hands have stayed low as the ball has not bounced very high.
3. The right foot has moved away from the stumps just far enough to give
the wicket-keeper balance as he gets his head into line.

you find it less tiring it is perfectly acceptable to adopt the same
stance as the slips.

The stance is the springboard from which the wicket-keeper
moves to take the ball. Do not, however, move too quickly.
You so often see wicket-keepers bobbing up and down as the
ball is bowled and then wondering why they cannot take it
cleanly. A batsman does not expect to time the ball well if he is
moving his head all over the place as he goes to hit it. Again,
the wicket-keeper is no different. If you are consistently failing
to get your timing right as a keeper, you are probably getting up
too early and then having to readjust to the bounce of the ball.
Try staying down in your stance position until the ball has

A splendid example of keeping down when the ball does not get up. The batsman has hit over the top of a long half-volley, and the wicket-keeper would have had little chance of a clean take if he had not kept his hands low.

pitched and then rise to take with the bounce. If the ball keeps low, you are in the right position to watch it all the way into your gloves. If it lifts, your leg and back muscles are primed to bring you up quickly with the ball. Those muscles are not geared to get you down as quickly. Even so, the initial movement to deal with the lifting ball does not bring these muscles into play. Keeping your head still, it is your arms which should cope with the bounce of the ball by bending at the elbows. The gloves are then in position to receive the ball, and only when the lift is too much to accommodate this movement will you actually come up with your body.

Apart from movement up and down, you will also have to

This wicket-keeper has got up far too soon and has taken his head out of line. The result is that the ball is on its way to the ground.

move from side to side as the bowlers stray wide of the stumps. There are two schools of thought relating to a wicket-keeper's lateral movements when standing up to the stumps. One advocates that the wicket-keeper moves within an imaginary semicircle going round behind the stumps. If you visualize his heels moving around the semicircle with the toes pointing in towards the wicket you get the idea of the movement suggested. The keeper's weight is always leaning in towards the wicket and so the hands can be quickly taken back to the bails to effect any stumping chance. On the other hand, a low snick which is not taken is likely to crash into the keeper's pads rather than carrying to slip, and there may be difficulties with the lifting ball wide of the stumps. The keeper can sometimes

Once the ball has been allowed to come into the gloves it is taken straight to the top of the stumps. Should the batsman have toppled forward, the bail is already off.

get a little cramped when, from a sideways-on position, he is taking a ball wide of the stumps which lifts above waist-high.

That is not the case with the other system of foot movement which involves taking the outside foot back from the crease to allow room for the hands to come up to take the ball almost as it passes. This might help you to take the wider, lifting balls more easily. If it seems to take longer to get the ball back to the stumps, that is only because it has been taken wider and therefore has further to travel. Also, because the keeper's outside foot has been taken out of the way, that low snick which he does not lay a glove on is more likely to pass unhindered through to the slips.

Whichever method is favoured, the biggest problem for the

wicket-keeper when standing up is the take down the leg-side. It is not easy to judge the behaviour of the ball for it is obscured by the batsman's body, often at the critical moment as it pitches. To counter this difficulty, the keeper should be moving into position to take down the leg-side, but should leave his head behind, as it were, to watch the ball for as long as

A good example of the wicket-keeper riding a bouncing ball. His gloves have come up with the ball and, by turning to get his body out of the way of his elbows, he could have accommodated even greater bounce.

Taking the ball down the leg-side.
1. The head is once again right behind the line of the ball.
2. His hands have kept low, and he has taken the ball in his right glove even though it is outside leg stump.
3. The left foot has moved across to take up the player's weight which is still leaning in towards the stumps.

This is a bad position in which to get when taking a ball down the leg-side. The left foot has gone so far back away from the stumps that all the wicket-keeper's weight has gone that way. Even when taking the ball cleanly it will mean a crucial delay in getting the ball back to the top of the stumps.

Not the way to take a ball down the leg-side when standing up to the wicket. There has been no foot movement and consequently the wicket-keeper's view is totally obscured by the batsman's body.

possible before it disappears from view behind the batsman. At this point, with his feet almost in position already, he can move his head quickly across to get the earliest possible view of the ball as it reappears. It is very important to stay down while completing this manoeuvre. There is only going to be a fraction of a second to sight the ball after it has passed the batsman down the leg-side. Don't waste any of it by having to get down again as well as across. As you move, it is essential that your head stays on the same plane, going across to the leg-side as if on runners.

When standing back, it is best to take initial half steps sideways to keep the chest on to the line of the approaching ball. Bring one foot alongside or cross it just behind the other before leading off again with the outside foot. Aim to get into

When the left foot does not go too far back behind the stumps, the wicket-keeper can take the ball down the leg-side and yet get it back quickly to the stumps because his weight is still favouring that direction.

position to take the ball straight in front of the body. However, it is not always possible to make enough ground in this way, especially if the ball has taken the edge and there is the chance of a catch. That is when it becomes necessary to dive.

There are some old men about who will tell you that good wicket-keepers don't have to dive. What they mean is, good wicket-keepers will move well enough to accept a lot of chances without needing to dive, while the poor keeper's footwork will have let him down so that the only way of getting even to simple chances is with a dive. There is nothing wrong with a wicket-keeper diving to take a chance that would not carry to another fielder or if there is no fielder there. It is not an admission of failure to expand the range of effectiveness.

To take the ball down the leg-side when standing back, the wicket-keeper has moved across while keeping his gloves low.

When he dives to right or left, the wicket-keeper is not merely launching himself in the general direction of the ball in the hope of a mid-air interception. If he does, he might well get a glove or two to the ball, but the chances of holding it as he crashes on to the ground in a heap are remote. There are two techniques for a diving take or catch—the two-handed and the one-handed. If you can get two hands to the ball, you should be turning in the air so that, having secured the ball in your gloves, you twist to ensure you land with your back to the bowler. So, if you are diving to your right, you take the ball in mid-air and turn your left shoulder under your body as you come down. This means that your hands are giving with the ball and cradling it up as you land. The impact on the ground is absorbed as you roll, and you should not jar the ball out of your grasp.

As the wicket-keeper dived to his right he got two hands to the ball. This time he twisted away from the stumps, riding with the ball, and has landed towards the back of his left shoulder.

It is similar with the one-handed take or when the ball is initially caught in one hand with the other glove closing over it. This usually happens when you are at full stretch with the ball perhaps falling a little short of you. In this case you will attempt to scoop the ball up and will turn the other shoulder under your body. Again, diving to your right, you get the glove under the ball and turn to land on the back of your right shoulder. Like most techniques in cricket you need to practise such actions until they become second nature, for you cannot afford the time to think about what you are doing while the ball is in the air.

Allowing your hands to give as you catch the ball is important in all circumstances – whether standing up or back, on your feet or diving, or even taking a return from the

A good catch when the ball was dropping just short and wide of the wicket-keeper. He has scooped the ball up with his right hand, and has twisted so that he lands on the back of his right shoulder rather than on his elbow, when the ball could be jerked out of his glove.

outfield. All wicket-keepers have a stronger hand, depending whether they are left- or right-handed, and will always endeavour to take the ball in the cup of that hand as they close the other glove over it. Contrary to uninformed opinion, they do not aim to catch the ball in both gloves at the same time. If they did, it would mean taking the ball in the join between the gloves and that crack is the weakest point of the assembly. Whichever is your dominant hand, allow it to give just a little as you take the ball before either taking it back to the top of the stumps or claiming the catch. This helps the ball to come to you and prevents your snatching at it. Never point your fingers towards the ball. In whatever direction your fingers point, always ensure that the backs of your gloves are at right angles to the line of the approaching ball.

One other point about the actual take. Wicket-keepers talk about having 'long arms'. This does not mean that they measure an excessive distance from shoulder to wrist. It means that they like to have their arms straight when taking the ball. Not ramrod stiff, but relaxed and straight. Then, as their hands give with the ball, there is no danger of the elbows getting caught up against the chest and the ball jarring out.

The wicket-keeper is without doubt the most important fielder in the side. As such, he shoulders much of the responsibility for setting the fielding standard and he has to work harder at his game than any of the other fielders to ensure the standard is high. But nobody else gets as much out of the game as the wicket-keeper on a day-to-day basis. He is always at the centre of the action and, because he so often determines the direction the action takes, his is a most privileged position.

It is a position that demands specialist practice and training. At a practice session, he should spend half an hour in the net with slow bowlers. This will be enough for him, so he then goes to the outfield, taking throws from fielders in the deep. By now he will be ready for his turn at the batting net for twenty minutes. Finally, when everyone else goes to change, the keeper will ask a bowler and batsman to stay behind with him. The batsman deliberately plays and misses so that the wicket-keeper gets a further twenty minutes concentrated taking practice.

FIELDING

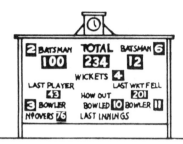

It is not only catches that win matches. They help considerably, but it is an all-round quality of fielding that makes the difference between two otherwise well-matched teams. You still hear discussions as to whether modern bowlers are quicker than their predecessors, or whether batsmen today are better than those in the history books. Whatever your viewpoint, you have to acknowledge that the basic methods of bowling and batting have remained relatively unchanged since the game evolved in its present form. The same cannot be said of fielding. It was not so very long ago that even county teams had only two or three fielders who could throw directly to the wicket-keeper from the boundary. Now everybody in a club side expects to do so. Fielding has unquestionably improved out of all recognition in the modern game; and not only have the standards shot up, the techniques themselves have also been expanded.

There used to be talk of attacking and defensive fielding techniques. While it is true to say that there are times when your first requirement is to stop the ball and others when your priority is to run the batsman out, you should have an attacking attitude the whole time in the field. Always be positive; want the ball to come to you so that you can show what a good fielder you are. By fielding well you can make a really useful contribution to the team. If you spend your time in the field hoping that the ball goes somewhere else and counting down the overs until the next interval you are not playing a positive role in the team. If you can get everyone to take pride in fielding performance, there will be a dramatic improvement, and you will be part of that winning team.

Again, going back not very many years, there would be specialists who would only field in certain positions. George fielded first slip, James hared around the boundary. Such fielders, of course, still exist but nowadays they also have to be all-rounders in the field. In the modern game, George may be a good slip, but he must also be able to sprint after the ball which is heading towards the unguarded third man boundary and send in a fast, straight throw to the wicket-keeper. The only way to develop these fielding skills is through practice. By practising purposefully and hard, everybody can at least become competent in the field and the most gifted natural fielders can become quite outstanding.

CATCHING

The greatest hindrance to most reasonably co-ordinated cricketers who are sound of limb is a fear of dropping the ball. When the hands become rigid with trepidation, even the simple chance can pop out. It can be frustrating and annoying for the bowler and other members of the side when a catch does go down; but nobody ever drops a catch on purpose, and everybody, at some stage, will drop a catch he really should have held. Bearing this in mind, fielders should be able to relax as the ball comes to them in the air and so will hold on to a greater number of chances. The more success they have, the more they will want to go for, and eventually bring off those spectacular efforts which turn matches. There are always situations in which fielders can decide whether to go for an unlikely catch or stand back to make it appear not to be a chance. Unless the position in a particular match demands that run-saving is more important than taking wickets, go for everything. You will drop a few because you have made difficult chances which a lesser fielder would not have got to at all. On the other hand, it is surprising just how many great catches you will hold if you have the determination to get at least one hand to anything in the air.

There are three main categories of catch. There is the type held close to the wicket, in the slips, at short leg and the like. There is the high catch hit to the outfield or skied to the single

Both slip and gully are in a good position should a catch come their way.
They are low down, even though slip has come up a little with the ball, and
they are comfortably balanced and have their eyes level. It appears that slip
has been watching the ball all the way while gully's eyes are fixed on the
edge of the bat.

saving position. And there is the well-hit skimming catch that
comes hard and straight to fielders in the ring. Each has its own
technique and each should be attempted in a positive, relaxed
frame of mind.

Statistically, most catches are offered to the close fielders.
Any list of catchers will usually be topped by the specialist slip.
Very many of the qualities associated with a wicket-keeper are
required by the slips. They have to be relaxed and yet
concentrating on every ball, expecting it to find the outside
edge and come to them. Just like the keeper, they should stay
low in their crouching position, ready to move in any direction
but not before they have sighted the ball. The distance they
stand from the bat is determined by the pace of the bowler, the

A good job the ball was not edged to slip or gully. Slip is hardly in a good position with his legs so wide apart that he will be unable to move quickly. Furthermore, his hands are apart and his elbows are resting on his knees. Meanwhile, gully has got up far too early.

pitch and the bounce. In general, because the ball will be slowed by a thicker deflection, second and third slips go a little closer and gully closer still. The space between them will be gauged by each deciding what area he can cover. Then they close up just a little so that there is no danger of a ball passing unhindered between them in the air. Gully is a little different in that he is generally on his own waiting for the really thick edge. When he holds on to a deliberate shot, it is a bonus.

As a slip fielder, you should stand with the weight on the balls of your feet which should be comfortably spaced so as to permit quick movement in either direction. If your weight drops back on to the heels, you are going to have problems. Some catches will come to you where you are, others will

143

A well-taken catch at short-leg. He has stayed down and watched the ball all the way into his hands, which have given with the ball.

require you to move forward. A slip rarely has to move back for a conventional catch; so it is important to be in a position to go forward. Keep your head still and eyes level, and never point your fingers at the ball. Let it come into your cupped hands.

Most first slips watch the ball all the way from the bowler's hand. It is possible to do this and still react to the thin deflection off the edge of the bat. Further round the slip cordon, however, where deflections are at a greater angle, it is advisable to watch the edge of the bat. Certainly in the gully there is no chance of adjusting your view from the ball leaving the bowler's hand and then reacting to the sharp change of angle off the bat. It is far better to watch the bat and even the batsman to get a few clues from his movements as to where the ball is likely to go.

It is the same when fielding at short-leg or at silly point. You cannot watch the ball all the way, and have to be watching the bat and the batsman. As well as being ready to take any chance which comes off the bat or bat and pad, you will be looking for early indications as to when evasive action is necessary. If you are close in at bat/pad on the off-side and see the batsman winding up to crash a wide half-volley to the cover boundary, don't try to deal with that delivery. It is far better for cover point to retrieve the ball from the boundary than for you to need the services of a surgeon!

Many fielders say they prefer to go close to the wicket because they do not have time to think about the catches coming to them, not fancying the skied shot for which they have to wait in the outfield. Yet, if you give yourself the best possible chance, there is no reason why you should not accept ninety-nine per cent of such chances.

The first requirement, of course, is to get right underneath the ball. There is a tendency for boundary fielders to see the ball hit in the air and to race towards it. The scramble back to the original position as the ball bounces once and goes over the boundary is one of the more embarrassing occurrences on a

The fielder looks well-set to take a high catch. He has taken up a good position under the ball, he is watching it carefully and has his hands above the level of his eyes. His little fingers and the heels of his hands are butted together to present a large cup for the ball to drop into and, with his elbows comfortably apart, there should be no danger of them crashing into his chest as he takes the ball. Had they been liable to get entangled with his body, the ball could be jerked out of his hands.

The alternative way to take a high catch, with the cup reversed so that the thumbs come together. As the catch is taken, the hands give and the head will be taken out of the way as hands come to rest near the shoulder.

cricket field. It is far easier to run in than to reverse, so give yourself a moment to see where the ball is coming before moving. Then move to the right place and, if there is time, steady yourself and relax your hands before taking the catch.

There are two ways of cupping your hands for such a catch. One is the conventional way with the little fingers touching and the fingers pointing away from your body, parallel to the ground. The other is with the thumbs touching and the fingers pointing back towards you—the reverse cup. Whichever way you feel comfortable is best for you. In either case, try to take the ball high. This is for two reasons. If you take it down by your chest or even lower, the ball flashes straight past your eyes and you cannot watch it right into your hands. You can if your hands catch the ball above eye-level. Secondly, if you do fumble the chance and the ball bounces out, there is a second

This fielder does not instil confidence that he is about to hold on to a high catch. He is off-balance, having failed to get right under the ball, and is trying to catch it far too low down. It will be impossible to get a second chance if it pops out when trying to catch it this low down.

The fielder taking this skimming catch has watched the ball all the way into his hands. The thumbs have been butted together in a reversed cup and are giving with the ball.

At the completion of a skimming catch to the fielder's left, he has let his hands come to rest on his shoulder and has moved his head out of the way as he did so.

chance to retrieve it. Drop it at waist height and the ball is on the ground before you can do anything about it. If you drop it when it is still above your eye-level, you can see what has happened and have a fraction longer to react and try again before it is grounded.

Assuming that you do take it at the first attempt, make sure that you allow your hands to give as the ball comes into them. However, take care that in doing so you don't let your elbows bump into your chest. Open your elbows to let them pass down outside your body so that there is no danger of the ball being jarred out of your hands.

A little give is also important when trying to take the hard, skimming catch. These often come anywhere in an arc from cover to mid-wicket and frequently arrive at head height. You do not have problems then with the trajectory, for the ball is travelling straight. If possible, get your head behind it with your hands cupped and the fingers pointing straight up. As you catch the ball, take your head out of the line just in case it finds a way through your hands, and let your hands give just past your ear.

GROUND FIELDING

As already mentioned, there are times when your priority is merely to prevent the ball from going for runs, others when you are trying to run the batsman out. However, even when you are simply attempting to stop the ball getting past you, you should still aim to do so as quickly as possible. For instance, the so-called long barrier is designed to be the most certain way to prevent a ball getting past you; but you don't want to take longer than necessary before getting the ball back over the top of the stumps.

The barrier technique is most often used in the outfield when the ball is hit along the ground. The batsmen are likely to complete an unhurried single, while there is little or no hope of running them out. You therefore want to make absolutely certain that there is no risk of the ball going past you for a boundary. To offer as much resistance as possible, you construct a barrier by going down on one knee so that there is a foot and leg along the ground and all your body above it. The ball will only get past if you misjudge its line or it takes an enormous deviation.

A fine example of the long barrier.

1. The head is right over the line of the ball.

2. The hands have come together to take the ball just in front of the body directly under the eyes.

3. Being a right-handed thrower, this fielder has gone down on to his left knee so that he can rise into a throwing position. The left knee butts up against the right heel so that there is no possibility of the ball getting through a gap.

With a long barrier like this, there is little point in getting the knee of his trousers dirty.

1. His head is nowhere near the line of the ball.

2. His hands are not together.

3. As a right-handed thrower he has gone down on to the wrong knee and left a huge gap between knee and heel.

Even when using the long barrier, do not wait for the ball to come to you. As soon as you have gauged the line, go to meet it so that your head is directly over the line of the oncoming ball. With your fingers pointing straight down, drop to one knee. If you are a right-handed thrower, it is best to use the left knee so that you are in a position to get straight up to throw. The knee should go down touching the right heel to form the barrier at right angles to the line of the ball. Make sure there are no gaps in the barrier. If there is a large hole between knee and heel, and the ball bobbles over your hands from a rough outfield, it will go straight through.

Some players, especially youngsters, appear embarrassed by going down into a long barrier, apparently seeing it as unnecessarily flamboyant. This is far from the case on anything other than an immaculately manicured outfield. They should be encouraged to take pride in their fielding and to adopt the correct, safest technique to deal with that particular situation.

The long barrier can be employed anywhere on the field, but when closer in it is likely that you will be trying to get a run-

The fielder has moved in to intercept the ball. As he reached it he turned sideways to pick up the ball in two hands under his head. From this position he will bring his right foot through in front of his body and can then return the ball.

out. The priority is to get the ball in as quickly as possible, so there is no time to take the safety first approach. Now you will be moving to intercept the ball at the first opportunity, although if you can get a foot behind your hand it can serve as a second line of defence. Again, you want your head right over the line of the ball to watch it into your hands. Having picked up on the move, you will already be turning sideways on to the target so that you are almost in a throwing position as you collect. Ideally, you have positioned yourself to pick up the ball under the shoulder you use to throw. Then there is no need to adjust your position before returning the ball to the keeper.

With the fast, underhand throw from the single-saving positions, there is no time at all to adjust your position to throw, or even to get two hands to the ball. Speed is absolutely of the essence in this situation. The ball may have been pushed a little way from the bat and as the batsmen set off for a single the fielder comes racing in, picks the ball up and in one movement has it back to the stumps. Even at high speed, the

This time the fielder has almost reached the ball, yet he is still in an upright position. To pick up the ball, he will have to bob down as it reaches him. He might well miss it altogether, or if he does pick it up, he is likely to bob back up himself as he throws it, sending it high over the target.

The fielder is moving in to pick up the ball and send an underhand return to the stumps. Although he is still some way from the approaching ball, he is already starting to get down and is going to the ball.

He picks up alongside his right foot, on the run, with his head over the line of the ball and watches it right into his hand.

Once the ball is in his hand, he releases it in the next stride. Although he has sent in the return, he has still not come up out of the running crouch and his head is low as it follows the line of the ball.

fielder should try to get his pacing right so that if he is a right-handed thrower, he picks the ball up on the outside of his right foot.

The key to this movement is getting the trunk and head low early. So many times you see a fielder rush in, dip down to pick up the ball and throw it as he bobs up again. Invariably it flies high over the wicket-keeper's head. As you race in, get low early, watch the ball right into your hand, throw on the run with an underhand movement, and don't allow yourself to come up until the ball has gone. In the old days it was thought to be quite something to get the ball back quickly to the keeper's gloves. Nowadays, as often as not, you should be aiming to hit the stumps so as to save the vital millisecond between the keeper taking your return and breaking the wicket.

Having chased after the ball, the fielder picks it up outside his foot. Being a right-handed thrower, he will turn to his left as soon as he can halt his momentum and send in his return.

The fielders will not be able to stop every ball. Some will get through the gaps and have to be chased. Just as with catching, go for everything. However well-struck the shot, the ball might go through a patch of lusher grass in the outfield and then take a couple of bumps and slow up considerably. When you reach the ball, there is well-established theory as to how it should be picked up. If it has stopped or is only moving slowly, the right-handed thrower picks the ball up alongside the inside of the left foot. He then stops himself with his weight on that foot, pushes off from it and throws as he transfers his weight over the right foot and back on to the left. The theory for retrieving the ball which is travelling at a greater pace is to pick it up outside the right foot, brake on that foot and push off it into the throw. In practice, you should aim to get to the ball as quickly as possible, pick it up at the first opportunity and get the thing in the air as soon as you can.

If the fielder turns the wrong way having picked up the ball, this is what happens. He has to turn through 360 degrees before he can throw it and vital moments are lost.

Having chased after the ball, this fielder has picked up and in so doing has leapt into a turn from which he sends in his return. As he turns in mid-air, his front arm is already seeking out the target.

Getting the ball in the air is an important consideration with all throws from the deep. Even if it is not the most accurate of throws, once the batsmen see the ball coming back to the wicket they are unlikely to go for a further run. If you take time in getting balanced, winding up and measuring a perfect return, they might. Some really athletic fielders can pick the ball up and jump into a turn from which they can throw while still in the air. Others have to brake, turn and throw. Either way, bear in mind that the best return is an early one.

It is only comparitively recently that outfielders have been seen diving and sliding. Gone are the days when the boundary fielder's last despairing effort was the outstretched boot. Nowadays you see fielders diving head-first for the ball, or intercepting it as it is about to cross the boundary by overtaking it while in mid-slide and flicking it back. A key

Having chased the ball to the boundary, the fielder slides past it and flicks it back as he crosses the line before getting up to return it.

The sliding interception. Rather than attempting to bend from the waist while running at speed, the fielder has slid on his left knee which is tucked under him.

As soon as he has picked up the ball on the slide, he throws while still on the ground. Even so, he keeps his head upright, cocks his throwing wrist, and points at the target with his front arm.

member of the side who risks injury by attempting such a stop if he cannot really do it is perhaps being foolish. If you have mastered the technique, you can save some vital runs by doing it. Moreover, such acrobatics need not be confined to the boundary. Many fielders can move to either side and instead of bending at the waist—a difficult operation on the run—tuck one knee under the body, time their slide to intercept the ball, and then throw as they rise. So if you move to your right, you tuck the left knee under you and stick out your right leg, almost as if going into a sliding tackle in soccer. The difference is that you keep your body upright to get your hands to the ball, and once it is safely collected, the throw is on its way.

Throughout this section on ground fielding, mention has been made of the throw without describing a throwing technique. Many players fail to appreciate that there is a technique for throwing just as there is for every other

The way to throw from the outfield.
1. The head is upright to get a good sight of the target.
2. The throwing arm is drawn back and the wrist cocked, with the ball held in the fingers.
3. The front arm is pointing directly at the target.
4. From a sideways position, the weight is just about to be transferred from the back foot over the front foot.

department of the game. The basic bowling action requires you to be sideways-on to the target, to use your non-bowling arm as a guide, and to release the ball as your weight transfers from back foot to front. The same principles apply to throwing.

Before throwing, if you are right-handed, get sideways-on, your left side directed at the target. With your weight on the right leg, point at the target with your left hand. It is surprising how much more accurate that simple action makes your throw. Then as your weight transfers to your left leg, your right arm whips through and releases the ball prior to the follow-through.

Fielders who throw the ball superbly are often commended for their 'strong arm'. Rather than great strength, they probably have a good throwing action and certainly excellent timing. Very supple players can reach the wicket from the boundary with hardly more than a round-arm flick of the wrist.

A bad position from which to throw.
1. The head is leaning right over.
2. There can be no use of the front arm.
3. The fielder is off balance and so is likely to lose power and accuracy.

Others have to get a little more leverage into their action by opening up to become rather more chest-on to the target as their arm comes more over the top. Their throws tend to lob higher and take longer to arrive than those of the flat throwers.

A good throw does not just happen. You have to work at it. Practice will increase your length of throw. Once you can throw the ball the required distance, try to improve your speed so that you can get the same distance but on a flatter trajectory. If you work on your accuracy as well, you will be on the way to becoming a top-class performer.

EXTRAS

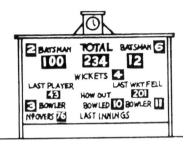

Cricket, fundamentally, is a simple game. The best players are those who consistently perform the basic elements better than anybody else. In the higher echelons of the game, matters, of course, get more complex. It is this complexity which contributes to cricket's esoteric charm. To the outsider, the game can appear to be slow and boring. But the more you understand about it, the more it fascinates and the more it can be enjoyed by player and spectator alike. So the aim of this chapter is to explain some of those finer points and mysteries, often overlooked, which are an aid to fuller understanding and appreciation of the game.

PITCHES

At the time of writing, only one British Prime Minister has appeared in first-class cricket. Sir Alex Douglas-Home, later Lord Home of the Hirsel, was Lord Dunglass when he appeared for Oxford University and Middlesex. He retained his love of the game throughout his time in high office, and tells a delightful story of one of his headmasters at Eton. Canon the Hon. Edward Lyttleton had himself played for Cambridge University and Middlesex before entering the Church. He too loved cricket so much that, as he confessed to Lord Home, he could not walk up the nave of his cathedral 'without speculating whether it would take spin or not'.

Cricket pitches should be easier to read than cathedral naves, yet a great mystique has developed about the way twenty-two yards of turf will respond to contact with a cricket ball. W.G. Grace is credited with the statement: 'There are some pitches on which it is always advisable to bat first on winning the toss. There are others upon which you have to think for a considerable length of time before electing to bat first.' John Tyldesley, when coach to Lancashire at the beginning of the century, was asked for advice by an amateur captain as to what to do if he won the toss on a particularly green-looking pitch. 'I think I'd bat before the flowers bloom,' was his reported reply.

Even experienced captains can misread a pitch and so it is a good idea to take the advice of other members of the side before making a decision. The opening batsmen and bowlers will be those who have to operate first on it, so their opinions on the pitch can be valuable. Even then, the captain has to consider the strengths and weaknesses of his side before deciding whether to bat or field first. Has he got a balanced attack capable of bowling out the opposition? Does the side do better chasing or defending a target? All are factors that must affect his decision.

You often hear people referring to a good pitch. The chances are they mean a good batting pitch, for it will probably present a stern test for the bowlers. They will get little help from the surface and will have to work extremely hard for any reward. But what constitutes a good batting pitch? It will have a firmness which produces an even bounce and a smooth texture, almost a sheen, which results in an even pace. There will be no tinge of green because most of the grass will have been shaved off, yet there is still that hard, even texture to the surface. The good-length ball from a medium pacer will consistently hit the top of the stumps. Such a pitch will always be dry. If you win the toss on one of these, all other considerations aside, you follow W.G. Grace's advice and have no hesitation in batting.

If the pitch has moisture in the surface, it will in all likelihood help the seam bowlers, because the surface will be soft enough to accept the seam on impact. Thus the bowler should be able to achieve a certain amount of deviation. If you win the toss on such a pitch, you do not automatically field first. You have to consider just how much moisture there is and how long it will remain there. In a match played on a hot, sunny day, a little moisture on the surface at the start will soon disappear, and you will be left with a good batting surface. On the other hand, if it is unlikely to dry out quickly, the pitch might not improve during the course of the game and you would still be advised to make first use of it.

When the pitch is really wet, the surface becomes pock-marked every time the ball lands. It is a surface which will help the medium pace cutter and orthodox spin bowler, but that does not always mean it is advisable to bowl first. You have to consider whether or not the pitch is going to get worse for batting as the match progresses. It might become so pock-marked that the ball will behave in a totally unpredictable way or, even worse, the surface might dry so that the marks cannot be rolled out and you have an impossible surface on which to bat. In such wet conditions the faster bowlers very often have difficulty in standing up while the spinners cannot grip the ball. If this is the case, it might be an idea to bat first in the hope that you can get 30 or 40 before conditions get too bad and then, as batting becomes harder and harder, go for all the runs available. You know it is going to be worse for the side that bats second. On the other hand, you might get bowled out for 60 and the opposition get them off the edge. There cannot be hard and fast rules.

An excessively green, well-grassed pitch will offer help to the faster bowlers in the form of movement off the seam. An under-prepared pitch will also have the bowlers rubbing their hands in anticipation. This is usually a pitch that has not been sufficiently rolled, resulting in a lack of compaction and therefore an uneven surface. If the ball hits a more solid area of the pitch it will lift, whereas if it makes impact on the softer sections it tends to keep low. It is very difficult to bat well on a pitch that lacks uniformity, for with the unpredictable bounce bowlers only have to deliver a straight ball to the other end to get wickets. There is no great art to bowling when one ball runs along the ground and the next, pitching close to the previous delivery, explodes off the pitch. In this instance it might be worth putting the other side in to bat, for it is easier, psychologically, to chase a low total that defend one. On the other hand, your bowlers might bowl badly, one of the opposition may throw the bat and get away with it, and you are chasing a total far larger than the pitch warrants. That's cricket!

Another type of under-prepared pitch is the one that may have been rolled but which lacks water. It will be dry, cracked and dusty. The ball is liable to keep low because of the crumbly nature of the surface which lacks cohesion. On the other hand, if it has been firm but then dries out excessively, the odd ball may really bite and lift. On the low turner, where the broken surface helps the spinner by allowing more friction to the ball, batsmen have to graft and work for their runs. In general, it is advisable to bat first before it gets any worse.

On a pitch that is drying out rapidly, it might be better to bowl first so that the opposition has to bat while it is at its worst, and your side can bat when the ball is behaving rather better. Batting is never easy when the ball is bouncing high, and when that bounce is unpredictable and there is lateral movement as well, the problems increase proportionately. With the odds stacked heavily against the batsman like this, it is time to attack the bowlers because, in effect, each run is worth more. Having said that, risks should be calculated. Straight balls should be treated with respect, but it becomes worth going for anything off the stumps. This does not mean having a monumental slog, but playing into the gaps. Many of the gaps will be in the air, especially if the field has closed in for catches near the wicket. Be prepared to hit the ball over the top, making sure you go right through with the shot. If you chase runs sensibly, and it is your day, you could end up a hero.

USE OF ROLLERS

From time to time there are regulations restricting the use of rollers at various stages of the match. However, given a free choice before you have to bat, what type of roller should you ask for? That rather depends on the sort of pitch you are playing on.

As in most other aspects of the game, there has to be a degree of personal judgement, with guidelines rather than hard and fast rules. However, as a generalization, if you are playing on a wet pitch you will want to use the heaviest roller available for as long as the regulations permit. This will have the effect of firming the pitch up and smoothing out any indentations. In the opposite situation, on a dusty, cracking pitch, you might be advised not to roll it at all. Any rolling might break it up even more, so just a brush to sweep away any debris and loose pieces would be the best preparation. On a really good batting pitch, as described earlier, a brush and a light roller are all that is required. That type of rolling will simply restore the sheen without disturbing the surface, and there is no point in altering conditions that are so favourable.

The difficulty comes when you are playing on a pitch which has had moisture but is now drying out. Then you have to ask yourself what the pitch was doing at the end of the previous innings. If the pitch was beginning to play better and better, with perhaps the tail-enders picking up quite useful scores, allow nature to take its course. Only use a light roller to smooth out the surface, for a heavy roller might bring up extra moisture and cause fresh problems. If, however, there was no noticeable improvement towards the end of the previous innings, use as heavy a roller as possible. This should flatten out the pitch and result in a more even pace and bounce.

BOWLING CHANGES

If your opening bowlers can dismiss the opposition in somewhere around twenty overs, you will not have to make any bowling changes. Alas, attacks are seldom as potent as that and so changes have to be made. Even if they do run through the opposition, the opening bowlers will have had to decide at which end each should bowl. That is usually quite simple in that the senior bowler in terms of penetrative potential will have choice of ends. So the quicker of the two opening bowlers will as a rule come downhill with the wind. This tends to produce a breed of very useful performers who can adapt to the less favourable conditions at the opposite end but who invariably develop into extremely effective bowlers.

Presuming that the opposition have not been bowled out, the time comes when a change has to be made. The good captain can judge which of his bowlers is in form and will get him into the attack. He also has to have the happy knack of taking a bowler out of the attack the over before he becomes a liability. Obviously a change is necessary if the bowler has just been hit for eighteen in an over. The canny captain will have eased him out of the attack while his figures were still respectable. In fact, there are ways of knowing when a bowler has passed his best. Apart from the obvious signs of tiredness, and talking to the bowler himself, the captain can keep in touch with the wicket-keeper. The latter can tell when the ball from the quicker bowlers no longer comes into the gloves with the same momentum; and he will indicate when the spinner has stopped turning the ball because of tired or sore fingers. When such a situation occurs or when the batsmen are no longer in any sort of discomfort, make a change.

There are some captains, particularly in the lower levels of the game, who appear to have decided the previous Thursday in what order the bowlers will come into the attack. Making no allowance for conditions or the opposition, they just know that Dave and Mike will open the bowling, John will be first change, Fred will deliver his off-breaks and George might get on for a short spell before the openers come back. It is bad enough having a rigid batting order that takes no account of the match situation. A fixed bowling order is utter nonsense, and no captain should go into the field with rigid ideas. He can have a plan, but it must be totally flexible.

The captain's early thinking is governed by what type of bowler he thinks will respond best on a particular surface or against a certain batsman. His aim is to put on the best bowlers for that situation as soon as possible. The captain should know which members of his attack perform best on good pitches and which will get most from favourable bowling conditions. They are not always the same men. Some bowlers fail to use conditions which should suit them. The type who tries too hard or who expects the pitch to do it all is rarely successful. Then there is the fast bowler who finds a pitch with a bit of life in it and whacks everything in half-way down the pitch. He enjoys seeing the batsman jumping about, but the good captain must quickly appreciate that the bowler is not going to hit the stumps too often.

This ability to choose the right bowler at the right time comes partly from knowing your own team and partly from assessing the batsmen. For instance, a left-handed batsman who is predominantly an on-side player might well be undone by an off-spinner, because he will always be trying to hit against the spin. Similarly, a right-handed on-side batsman can get into a lot of trouble against the left-arm spinner. If a right-handed batsman has a tendency to play inside out, get the inswing bowler or off-spinner up against him. The same type should prove effective against the off-side player who allows his head to drop off-balance when he gets a ball on middle and leg.

Discuss which end the bowler wants to bowl. Wind direction and a slope straight up and down the pitch will obviously affect the opener's choice of ends, but it also has an effect later. Use a cross wind to help the swing bowler, or a slope from one side of the square to the other to assist the spinner to turn the ball down the hill. Consider the presence of a short boundary on one side. The inswinger or off-break bowler will not want it on the leg-side of the right hander because he is moving the ball towards it. All the batsmen has to do then is help it on its way for four. As a general rule, the slow bowlers will not want a short boundary behind them, while the quicker bowlers will not want one behind the bat. Batsmen tend to get runs behind off the quicker bowlers and to hit the spinners back in front. Short boundaries in those directions can therefore prove to be unnecessarily expensive. Some slow bowlers like to bowl into the wind, because the batsman can be deceived by the ball held up in the air. On the other hand, many spinners like to force the batsman to hit into the wind, as it is that much harder to reach the straight boundary.

It is extremely important to discuss ends with the bowler. He is unlikely to give of his best at one end if he thinks the opposite end would suit him better. Logic might point to a certain bowler operating from the pavilion end. However, if he got wickets last year at the town end, he may feel more comfortable and bowl better from that end. If he doesn't, you can point out the obvious advantages to be enjoyed at the pavilion end and switch him. Communication is an essential quality for a captain, who should keep his bowlers informed about general strategy. He should tell a bowler that he wants him to keep an end tied up for the next half-dozen overs, or that he must go all out to get wickets and not mind the cost. He should inform the bowler that he has only one more over to bowl and, more importantly, tell a bowler when he is due to enter the attack so that he can get properly warmed-up.

FIELD PLACINGS

Cricket is sometimes envisaged as a game for individual encounters rather than a genuine team game. This is quite wrong. Only when the team in the field is operating as a single unit is it truly effective. The bowler against the batsman is the highlighted contest, but unless the fielders are supporting the bowler, that contest is heavily weighted in favour of the batsman; and in order for the fielders to be of maximum use, they must be stationed in the correct positions.

Just as there cannot be wholly rigid thinking to any aspect of the game, so you must keep an open mind about fielding positions. The reason why a number of recognized—and named—positions have evolved over the years is that in certain circumstances the ball has been found to travel frequently to that part of the field. However, those positions are only guidelines and it is necessary to react to the conditions operating at any given time. It is not a bad idea to set a conventional field for a certain type of bowler, but be prepared to adapt it to achieve your objective. For instance, if you discover that the ball is not swinging or turning as expected, you may not employ as many slips or short legs as usual. Or you might find that a certain batsman plays in a particular way, so that you require unconventional field placings to counter such unorthodox batting.

At all times think how best to exert pressure on the batsman. This does not necessarily mean just posting men in catching positions or cutting off the area in which the batsman is scoring most of his runs. Consider how you can dictate which batsman gets more of the strike. If a number three has 89 on the board and number ten is scratching about on 5, you have far more chance of a wicket and keeping the scoring down if you can keep number three away from the strike. When number ten is facing towards the end of an over, push the single-saving fielders back. Then he might get to the other end to face the whole of the next over. Similarly, reinforce the single-saving positions when number three has the strike towards the end of an over. You don't want him to face the next one.

There are also methods of making a batsman play in a way that gives the bowler the best chance of taking a wicket. Think about leaving gaps in the field to encourage the batsman to look for runs in a way which forces him to play dangerously. For instance, the off-break bowler might leave an obvious gap square with the wicket on the off-side. He will be hoping that the batsman will try to hit him into that area of the field in the search for runs. If he does, he will be playing right against the spin.

It is possible to exert pressure by controlling the scoring rate, thus inducing more risks by the batsman and consequently a better chance of taking wickets. If the batting side need more than five runs an over, their thoughts will be centred on getting a boundary in each over. If, towards the end of an over, they have scored only two singles, the need for a four will become more pressing. At that point it is worth giving the single but defending the most vulnerable boundaries. For instance, you might push mid-off and mid-on back to long-off and long-on. The batsman is then likely to get only a single and the team will fall further behind the required rate.

One other point on field placing. Remember that you cannot set a field for a bad ball. Some captains panic and have fielders chasing all over the parish after any ball is hit to the boundary. You only have nine men to deploy, so use them sensibly. If your left-arm spinner has been bowling well to six men on the off-side and three on the leg, don't suddenly post a deep square leg because he drops one short outside the leg stump and is pulled. If he goes on doing that it is time to take him off, not to try to accommodate that awful delivery.

The diagrams which follow are meant to give you a sound basis for setting a field to the most common types of bowler in conditions which give him a little but not excessive help. It is presumed that, in each case, the batsman is right-handed. However, it is not difficult to cater for the left-hander simply by working out what the ball is doing to him. For example, the outswinger to the right-handed batsman will be an inswinger to the left-hander.

Away-swing bowler

This is a suggested field for the bowler of medium pace or above who moves the ball away from the right-handed batsman. As with all of these plans, it is a *suggested* field and not *the* field. So many variables apply that the captain and bowler between them have to decide what is right for any particular situation. In this instance there are two slips (1 and 2) and a gully (3) for the catch off the outside edge. To give the ball every opportunity to swing, the bowler will want to keep it to a full length. This means that he should be protected from punishment on the off-side as far as possible should he overpitch, hence the point (4), cover (5) and mid-off (6) saving the single. Mid-on (7) and mid-wicket (8) perform similar duties on the leg side, while fine leg (9) guards against four runs from the ball straying down the leg-side.

When the captain wants to press the attack, he can reinforce the slip cordon from the covers, pushing mid-off wider to deal with the area of the field left unguarded. One or more of the leg-side fielders can be brought up into close catching positions as well. It should be remembered, however, that attacking does not always mean crowding the bat. If the ball is swinging but the batsman is still going for his shots, an extra man in the covers for the mishit drive might be more likely than short leg to take a catch. If the requirement is to defend rather than attack, get one of the close catchers to drop down to third man, and/or set a square leg, particularly if the ball is not swinging.

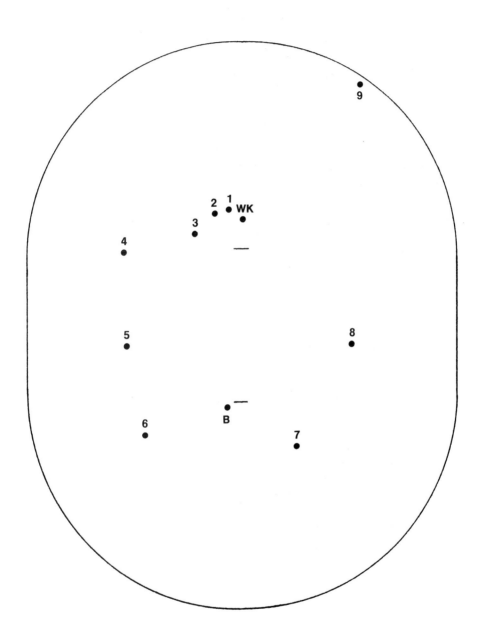

Inswing bowler

Even though the inswing bowler is moving the ball into the right-hander, he should still have a slip (1) for when the ball goes straight on or seams away off the pitch. The third man (2) can cover anything that beats slip, while the point (3) and mid-off (4) are there to save the single on the off-side. Because he is moving the ball in, the leg-side field is more populated than for the away-swing bowler. There are three men saving the single, mid-on (5), mid-wicket (6) and square leg (7), with the long leg (9) out, and a short leg (8) up for the catch.

As ever, the situation might demand more attacking fielders, with third man being brought up into the slips, as could long leg, and either square leg or mid-wicket going into bat/pad. He might well get a catch from the ball that finds the inside edge of the bat and bounces up off the pad if the batsman plays with bat and pad close together. If, however, he tends to push forward with his bat in advance of his pad, a leg slip might come into play. Defensive options for this type of bowler include dispensing with the close catchers to reinforce the covers or putting a man back on the leg-side boundary, depending on the bowler's line of attack.

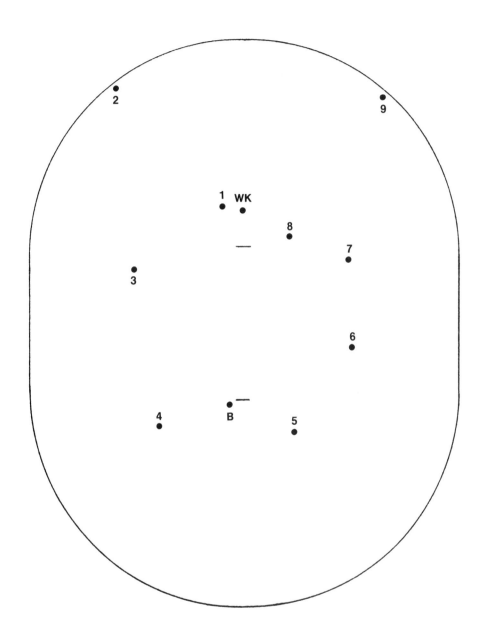

Off-spin bowler

Not much will go for runs behind the wicket with this type of bowler, so most of the fielders will be in front of the bat. A slip (1) can be used, particularly if the bowler can deliver an arm-ball that does not turn but drifts away from the bat. However, if the captain is looking to use his off-spinner in a containing role on a pitch that does not offer much help, the slip might have to drop down to backward point. Point (2), cover (3) and mid-off (4) will take care of the off-side with cover and mid-off fairly straight. This leaves a gap on the off-side to encourage the batsman to attempt a hit against the spin. Mid-on (5) and mid-wicket (6) should get plenty of work to do, with the deep square leg (9) to counter the sweep. The short legs (7 and 8) will be hoping for a straightforward inside leg or the chance that comes off bat and pad.

The short legs can be pushed back into defensive positions should the need arise, while mid-on and mid-off can also be positioned deeper as required. This is not always a purely defensive move. If the batsman is willing to have a go at hitting the bowler straight, place men in position for the mishit. However, if the ball is turning, you might post another short leg and bring a man up to bat/pad on the off-side.

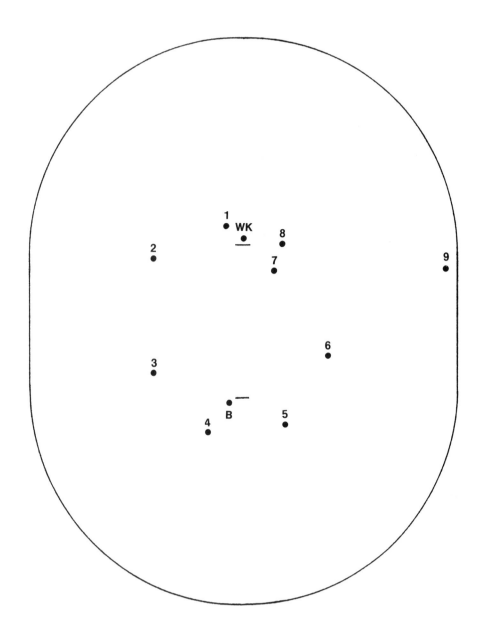

Leg-spin bowler

With the ball turning away from the right-handed batsman, the slip (1) is an important catching position. The point (2) is a little backward for the ball which is run down behind square on the off-side, and he is joined by the cover (3), extra-cover (4) and mid-off (5) to form the ring of fielders on the off. With the odd googly turning the other way and perhaps less dependable control from the leg-spin bowler, there are four men on the leg-side. Mid-on (6), mid-wicket (7) and square leg (8) cover the singles, while the short leg (9) is there for any catch resulting from the googly or when the batsman prods against the spin.

Leg-spinners are essentially attacking bowlers, and so when the ball is turning, a gully or silly point can be employed as an additional close catcher. As the ball turns away from the bat, any mishit is likely to go on the off-side. Therefore, if the leg-spinner is hit back over mid-off, it can sometimes be worthwhile leaving mid-off where he is to encourage the stroke, but put extra-cover deeper. Then, if the shot is not middled, it can spin out for the catch.

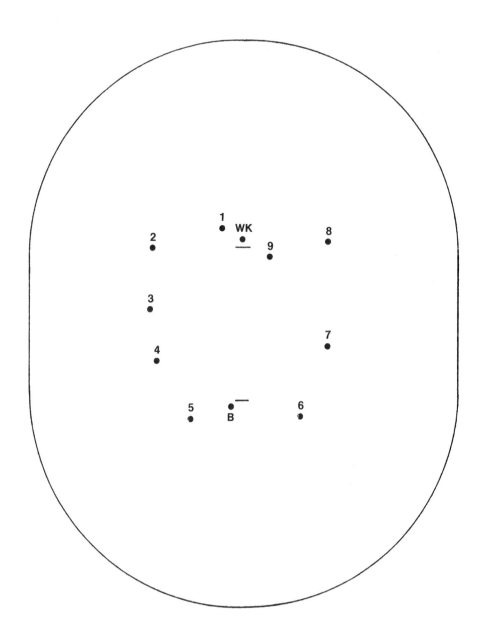

Left-arm spin bowler

Many of the same features apply to the field of the orthodox left-arm spinner as discussed for the leg-spinner. The slip (1) is in for the catch, while there is a ring of single-savers from backward point (2), point (3), cover (4), extra-cover (5) to mid-off (6). The mid-on (7), mid-wicket (8) and square leg (9) prevent singles on the leg-side.

On a turning pitch where the bowler is getting plenty of assistance, one of those leg-side fielders can be brought up to short-leg for the bat/pad chance from the arm-ball. Similarly the backward point could come into gully, while one of the covers could come up close on the off-side for the catch. When defensive considerations are paramount, one of his covers can be pushed back to the boundary, mid-off can go back, and the slip removed.

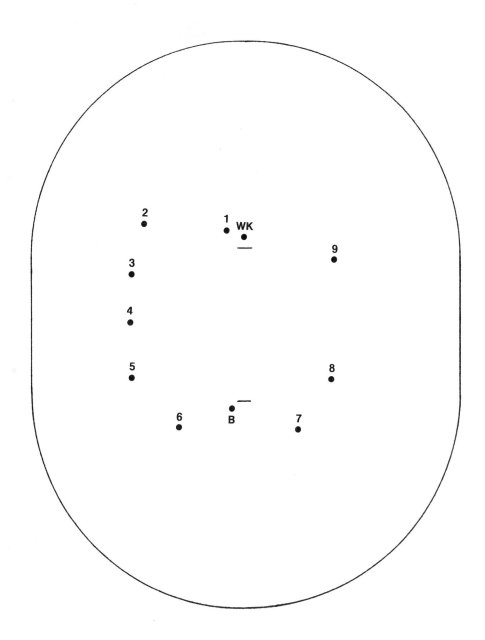

LEADERSHIP

Virtually all of this chapter has dealt with topics which should be of particular interest to the captain. But they are not intended exclusively for the captain, for the more all the team players know about the game, the better it is for everyone. The captain should be prepared to take informed advice on various matters. Accepting good advice and listening to ideas from senior members of the team is a sign of strength, not weakness. It is part of the ability to communicate—a vital quality in a captain.

The ultimate responsibility of the good captain might be summed up by saying that he needs to be a very competent manager who thoroughly understands cricket. He must be popular with his team, either because they like him as a person or because they respect him as a leader. The ideal combination of friendship and respect will get the rest of the side playing their best for him. This is not all one-way traffic. The captain has to communicate with the team so that each member knows exactly what is expected of him. Bowlers should understand the overall strategy and the part they have to play in it. When they are not bowling, they should be told when they are likely to get on. Batsmen out in the middle should be kept informed of the situation and of policy by a message system. When the batting order is changed to suit a particular situation, advise all concerned. Don't just instruct number nine to go in second wicket down to boost the scoring rate. Tell number four as well so that he knows why he is moving down the order, and that it is for tactical rather than disciplinary reasons.

Discipline is an integral part of leadership. It includes self-discipline, when the captain has to set the example by sticking unswervingly to the code of conduct he expects from the team. This includes standards of behaviour, appearance and punctuality, as well as things like fitness and practice. This discipline must apply to all members of the team. However, it is not only a question of reprimanding colleagues. The captain must get to know all of his team so that he can tell which of them need firm handling and which respond better to encouragement.

The captain may not be the best player in the side, but unless he can perform at the required level he is unlikely to earn the respect of his team. As well as a player and psychologist, he needs to be the manager, organizer, sympathizer, motivator, disciplinarian, leader, strategist, communicator, diplomat, selector, coach and, occasionally, nursemaid. This leadership business is not easy. It takes a particular type of person to relish such responsibility, and unless he enjoys it, he is unlikely to be much good at it. As with every other aspect of the game, the rewards of captaincy are proportionate to the effort expended. The effort is enormous, but think of those rewards.

The authors Les Lenham (*left*) and Ralph Dellor

INDEX

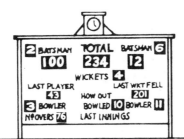